IS JESUS GOD?

Is Jesus God?

An Answer to Infidels in the Church and Out

By EVANGELIST JOHN R. RICE, D.D., LITT.D.

Author of *Prayer—Asking and Receiving; The Home: Court-
ship, Marriage and Children; Twelve Tremendous Themes;
The Ruin of a Christian; Revival Appeals,* etc.

Editor of THE SWORD OF THE LORD.

*Get this book into the hands of every modernist
and doubter possible.*

SWORD OF THE LORD PUBLISHERS
214 West Wesley Street   Wheaton, Illinois

CONTENTS

INTRODUCTION

Yes, Jesus is God! I believe the honest, inquiring heart will find here abundant evidence of that fact.

Unbelief in Christ and the Bible is not based on learning; it is based on sin. Modernists, Unitarians, infidels are not that because they are intelligent; they are that because they are rebels. When a man does not believe in Christ, it is not an honest, "I cannot," but it is a stubborn, "I will not." Jesus said: "And this is the condemnation, that light is come into the world, and men loved darkness rather than light, because their deeds were evil. For every one that doeth evil hateth the light, neither cometh to the light, lest his deeds should be reproved. But he that doeth truth cometh to the light, that his deeds may be made manifest, that they are wrought in God" (John 3:19-21). Here is the real explanation of all the unbelief in the world. Unbelief is grounded primarily in the will that is against God, not in the intelligence. There are no scientific or historical or philosophical facts which can make any honest inquirer turn from the Bible or from Christ. If men believe a system of thought and doctrine which denies the truth of the Bible and the deity of Christ, some wicked motive (an "evil heart of unbelief," as Hebrews 3:12 says), either consciously or unconsciously, entered into the decision to doubt and made them susceptible to temptation.

Hence the way to deal with unbelief is to deal with it as sin. The problems of infidelity are problems of the heart, not primarily of the mind. And that means that the way to deal with unbelievers is to preach to them the Word of God, preach to them as Christ-rejecting sinners who need salvation.

I learned from D. L. Moody and R. A. Torrey that infidels and atheists can often be won by compelling them honestly to face the Word of God. The late Mr. George Soltau says that D. L. Moody, about 1883, in East London reserved the giant tabernacle one Monday night for "atheists, skeptics and free-thinkers of all shades." Five thousand such men, led by Charles Bradlaugh, filled the hall and Moody preached to them. Soltau says: "From that night till the end of the week nearly two thousand men were swung out from the ranks of the foe into the army of the Lord, by the surrender of their will." The atheists' clubs never recovered their footing in England thereafter (See "Mr. Moody and the Free-Thinkers" in *The Sword Book of Treasures*).

Dr. R. A. Torrey won many an atheist and has given detailed suggestions for dealing with such unbelievers.

Christians should not be afraid of modernists. I remember how startled I was to read Tom Paine's *Age of Reason* and to find that the book, as first published, was written without the author's seeing or referring to either a Bible or Testament! Without any investigation of the Bible, Paine culled from other infidels what he could of argument against the Book he had never read but hated! Later he found it necessary to write a second part, and he says: "Under these disadvantages, I began the former part of the *Age of Reason;* I had, besides, neither Bible nor Testament to refer to, though I was writing against both; nor could I procure any: nothwithstanding which, I have produced a work that no Bible believer, though writing at his ease, and with a library of Church books about him, can refute." (!!!) And this second part of the book, written after he got out of jail in Luxembourg and with the Bible before him, abounds in mistakes and evidences of ignorance! You may be sure that unbelief always, in infidels, in the church or out, comes from bad hearts, without a solid foundation of fact.

Only one thing does an honest unbeliever need in order to learn the truth about whether or not Jesus is God. He needs an humble, inquiring heart, hungry for truth and righteousness which will cause him to investigate the claims of Christ and the Bible. One who does not have such an attitude of heart may scorn this book. Those who want to know the truth will, we trust, read it with real profit and pleasure. I hope that this book may be put into the hands of modernists, atheists and agnostics everywhere. It goes forth with much prayer.

These chapters were originally published in *The Sword of the Lord* of which I have the honor of being editor. I was impelled to put them into a book when one young pastor, trained in the schools of modernism, wrote how he had been gloriously restored to the faith of his childhood by some of these articles, and begged me to have them printed to strengthen other ministers who had been mistaught but were hungry for the truth.

May all who love the dear Lord Jesus be true to His gospel! And "if any man preach any other gospel unto you than that ye have received, let him be accursed" (Gal. 1:9). Yes, Jesus Christ is God!

In His dear name,

JOHN R. RICE

Wheaton, Illinois
December, 1947

Chapter 1

IS JESUS GOD?

New York Modernist Visiting Brooklyn Tent Evangel Does Not Believe in the Deity of Christ, Nor His Virgin Birth; Deplores the Teaching That Those Who Will Not Accept Christ As the Virgin-Born Saviour Go to Hell

In answer, the author shows that "the religion of Jesus," "the message of Jesus," and "the spirit of Jesus," involve (1) an infallible Bible, as Jesus regarded it; (2) the absolute necessity of a new birth, regeneration by faith in Christ; (3) the very deity of Christ Himself [Paul taught the deity of Christ, along with the four Gospels and the Old Testament]; (4) Modernism, denying the deity of Christ, is foretold in the Scriptures with solemn warnings to shun these insincere and wicked deceivers

In a tent revival campaign in Brooklyn, New York, during the month of July, a modernist came to hear me speak. He wrote a letter objecting to my clear teaching that one could not be saved who did not accept Christ as the very Son of God which He claimed to be. He objected to my saying that unbelievers in Christ were lost. He wrote saying that we should have "the spirit of Jesus," that we should preach "the message of Jesus," that after all, other things were not so essential and we should simply pattern after "the religion of Jesus." In his letter he asked that I answer some of his questions about the deity and virgin birth of Christ. He heard me again, and again wrote me.

After returning to Wheaton, I took time to write this man very carefully a long letter of many pages. Hoping that he was sincere and really wanted to know the truth, I answered his questions from the Bible, the Word of God.

It may be that some of the readers of this volume have been so unfortunate as to have listened to the teaching of modernists in the college or seminary classroom, or have been under the so-called "preaching" of modernists who do not believe the Bible and do not believe that Jesus is the Son of God. Or perhaps they have been reading a modernistic magazine of unbelief, like *The Christian Century;* or denominational Sunday School quarterlies put out by these subtle deniers of the faith, these false teachers, blind leaders of the blind, as Jesus called them; these "wolves in sheep's clothing," who pretend to be for God and Christ and the Bible but are actually enemies of Bible Christianity, enemies of the cross of Christ. Some of those who read may have heard the great fallacy that God is the Father of all and that all of us, whether converted or not, are children of God. You may have been taught that it does not matter whether one believes in the virgin birth and it does not matter whether you agree on the inspiration of the Bible and the blood atonement, just so you have "the spirit of Jesus" and walk in "the Jesus way."

Or you may have read the sermon by Harry Emerson Fosdick on "The Peril of Worshipping Jesus," in the book, *The Hope of the World,* sold in denominational book stores, God forgive them.

To all such I commend this letter, an honest Bible answer to a man who wanted the religion of Jesus and yet thought he could discard the inspiration of the Bible and even the deity and virgin birth of our Saviour, and still be a Christian!

Omitting the salutation and the first paragraph which was personal, explaining and apologizing for my delay in writing, here is my letter to the modernist:

The Religion of Jesus

In your first letter you said, "Would it not serve the kingdom's interests better if the church centered its attention more on the religion of Jesus, that is, the religion which Jesus Himself personally experienced . . .?" Again you said, "If the church would pattern its religion after the religion of Jesus and make the ideals and principles which He lived and taught dominant in its life, our world would soon be a very different place." You say that Christians should manifest "the spirit of Jesus" and you think I do not manifest that spirit in preaching that Jesus was born of a virgin, that the Bible is the infallible Word of God, that Jesus Himself is God come in the flesh. Again you say, "There seems to be a widespread failure to take Jesus Christ seriously," and you say that my preaching should be "the message of Jesus."

Now surely we can agree on this, that we ought to follow the teachings of Jesus and have the spirit of Jesus and the message of Jesus. If you are sincere in that position, all your other difficulties can be soon settled.

1. "The Religion of Jesus" Involves an Infallible Bible, Inspired of God and Wholly Reliable

It is very easy to find exactly how Jesus felt about the Bible. Listen to His words in Luke 24: 25-27,

"Then he said unto them, O fools, and slow of heart to believe all that the prophets have spoken: Ought not Christ to have suffered these things, and to enter into his glory? And beginning at Moses and all the prophets, he expounded unto them in all the scriptures the things concerning himself."

Here Jesus says (a) that one who is even slow to believe "all that the prophets have spoken" is a fool. (b) He says that the Old Testament clearly foretold that Christ would suffer these things and then enter into His glory. That involves supernatural revelation of the future. (c) Then He applied this statement about the infallibility of the Bible and "all that the prophets have spoken" to "Moses and all the prophets," and to "all the scriptures." Jesus, then, clearly teaches that all the Old Testament Scriptures are divinely inspired, and that any man who is even slow to believe them is a fool. That is the religion of Jesus about the Bible! The Bible is the authority, then, the *infallible* authority of Jesus Christ.

If anyone wants to preach the message of Jesus, here it is. The Bible contains the infallible revelation of the will of God, and anyone slow to believe it is a fool.

Every time this question came up, Jesus put Himself on record the same way. He called the Scriptures literally "every word that proceedeth out of the mouth of God" (Matt. 4: 4). That is literally word-for-word, or verbal inspiration of the Old Testament Scriptures. And one who accepts the absolute inspiration of the Old Testament Scriptures necessarily accepts the inspiration of the New.

Jesus claimed the divine authority of every jot and tittle of the law, saying, "Till heaven and earth pass, one jot or one tittle shall in no wise pass from the law, till all be fulfilled" (Matt. 5: 18).

Jesus Himself repeatedly quoted the Old Testament as the Word of God. He believed in the direct creation of man and woman, male and female, as described in the first chapters of Genesis (Matt. 19: 4, 5). Jesus Himself plainly said that in the days of Noah "Noe entered into the ark," and that "the flood came, and took them [the wicked outside the ark] all away" (Matt. 24: 38, 39). Jesus clearly authenticated the Genesis account of the flood.

Jesus believed also in the inspiration of the book of Jonah. He said, "For as Jonas was three days and three nights in the whale's belly; so shall the Son of man be three days and three nights in the heart of the earth" (Matt. 12: 40). And in the same connection He clearly said that His resurrection from the dead would be the sign of His deity.

If you have "the religion of Jesus," and if you preach "the message of Jesus," then you must preach that the Bible is the infallible Word of God, that anyone is a fool who is even slow to believe it—even that the accounts of direct creation, of the flood, of the miracle of Jonah and the whale, etc., happened exactly as the Old Testament records them.

Any man who pretends to preach the religion of Jesus, the message of Jesus, and to have the spirit of Jesus, and denies the authenticity and the authority of the Word of God, is an imposter.   He is either an ignoramus who never investigated the facts, or an insincere hypocrite who does not mean what he says, but with feigned words seeks to deceive the simple.   The religion of Jesus involves an infallible Bible.

Furthermore, what Jesus claimed for the Old Testament He claimed for the Gospels quoting His sayings. In Matthew 24: 35 He said, "Heaven and earth shall pass away, but my words shall not pass away."   That means that Jesus claimed His words would be infallibly recorded, never to be lost.   That certainly authenticates the Gospels.

However, I never knew of anyone except orthodox Jews who accepted the infallible inspiration of the Old Testament and denied the inspiration of the New, and even orthodox Jews cannot maintain their position if they really study the New Testament as well as the Old. When you prove the inspiration of the Old Testament, you have already accepted the Bible doctrine of inspiration, and the New Testament proves itself.

Here is the foundation of the doctrine of Jesus, the

message of Jesus. Here is the very heart of "the religion of Jesus," of "the spirit of Jesus." The religion of Jesus involves a supernaturally-inspired and infallible Bible. You must either discard the Bible and discard Jesus Christ with it, or you must accept the Bible and accept Jesus Christ with it. They are inseparable. The religion of Jesus Christ, His doctrine, His message, His spirit, are based on His absolute acceptance of the Scriptures as the Word of God, without error.

2. The Message of Jesus Christ Absolutely Demands a New Birth, Personal Regeneration by Faith in Christ's Atoning Death, and Jesus Repeatedly Consigned to Eternal Condemnation and Hell All Who Did Not Accept Him and Depend Upon Him as the Christ Revealed in the Old Testament, "the Lamb of God Which Taketh Away the Sin of the World"

You say in your second letter, "Calling those who differ with you in opinion and method of interpreting the Bible coarse and uncharitable names, and consigning them to Hell is, I feel, hardly manifesting the love of God and the spirit of the Master." Now certainly any man who sets up his own standards and, simply because others do not agree with his personal opinions, calls them "coarse and uncharitable names" and consigns them to Hell is doing wrong. Mark you, I said if a man makes his own standards, which he himself has invented and evolved, the only way to be saved, and consigns others to Hell. I assure you, I will never do that.

In this matter the message of Jesus Christ is the exact message of the rest of the Bible. Christ never went against the Bible. The Bible never goes against Jesus Christ. And so the message of Paul and the message of Jesus always agree. What did Jesus demand and require about individual regeneration, or the new birth? He said, "Except a man be born again, he cannot see the kingdom of God" (John 3: 3). "Except a man be born of water and of the Spirit, he cannot enter into the kingdom of God" (John 3: 5). "Marvel not that I said unto thee, Ye must be born again" (John 3: 7). "He that believeth on him is not condemned: but he that believeth not is condemned already, because he hath not believed in the name of the only begotten Son of God" (John 3: 18).

These Scriptures clearly show that Jesus had a clearcut doctrine on salvation. One who is born again, that is, has a supernatural change of heart, is saved. One who is not born again, who does not have a supernatural change of heart, is not saved and can never enter the kingdom of God; in fact, cannot even see that kingdom! That is the religion of Jesus.

And Jesus made it clear that the only possible way to have this change of heart, this new birth, was by personal faith in Jesus Christ Himself. He who has personally trusted Christ for forgiveness and salvation is not condemned but already has everlasting life, as Jesus said in John 3: 15; John 3: 16; John 5: 24 and John 6: 47. Sometimes there is slightly different language, sometimes the word *repent* is used, meaning a heart-turning from sin to Christ, instead of the word *believe;* but it is clear from the language of the Lord Jesus continually that He has in mind the same plan of salvation—the one taught throughout the whole Bible. So when one *comes* to Christ, he believes in Christ; when one repents of his sin or turns to Christ, then of course he is trusting in Christ. Those who do so personally accept Christ as Saviour and depend upon Him for salvation are saved, have everlasting life, are born again, are children of God. That is the clear teaching of Jesus, the message of Jesus, the religion of Jesus.

The message of Jesus, then, is not that all of us are naturally the children of God. The message of Jesus is not that all will get to Heaven. The clear teaching of Jesus Christ is that many people go to Hell, a place of torment. Jesus said, "Whosoever shall say, Thou fool, shall be in danger of hell fire" (Matt. 5: 22). He warned all not to fear them which were able to kill the body, "but rather fear him which is able to destroy both soul and body in hell" (Matt. 10: 28). He plainly foretold that He, the Son of man, would in the future "send forth his angels" to take out the wicked, "And shall cast them into a furnace of fire; there shall be wailing and gnashing of teeth" (Matt. 13: 41, 42). Again He said, "So shall it be at the end of the world: the angels shall come forth, and sever the wicked from among the just, And shall cast them into the furnace of fire: there shall be wailing and gnashing of teeth" (Matt. 13: 49, 50).

Jesus did not say that the moral, religious Pharisees were the children of God and His spiritual brothers. Because they did not believe in His deity and accept Him as the promised Messiah, the Lamb of God that takes away the sin of the world, He said to them, "Ye are of your father the devil, and the lusts of your father ye will do" (John 8: 44). It was to Nicodemus, a Pharisee, a church leader, as moral and upright and kindly as any modernist preacher in the world, that Jesus said, "Except a man be born again, he cannot see the kingdom of God" (John 3: 3). And, speaking to Pharisees and scribes as a party, especially moral and religious people, Jesus said, "Ye serpents, ye generation of vipers, how can ye escape the damnation of hell?" (Matt. 23: 33).

Any man, then, who preaches "the message of Jesus" and who has "the spirit of Jesus"; any man who believes as Jesus believed and preaches as Jesus preached, must plainly warn those who do not accept Him as God come in the flesh, those who have not personally depended upon Him for salvation, that they are going to Hell. That is not coarse, that is not uncharitable; that is "the spirit of Jesus" and "the religion of Jesus" and "the message of Jesus."

3. The Message and Doctrine of Jesus Was That He Himself Was Deity, Very God

Anybody who wants to practice the religion of Jesus must begin where Jesus began, must believe what Jesus believed, and teach what Jesus taught.

First, Jesus accepted Old Testament prophecies which declare the absolute deity of the coming Messiah, as referring to Himself. Isaiah 7: 14 says, "Therefore the Lord himself shall give you a sign; Behold, a virgin shall conceive, and bear a son, and shall call his name Immanuel." The Authorized Version, the Revised Version, the Twentieth Century New Testament, all in Matthew 1:23 quote this verse and translate the word "virgin" alike. Weymouth translation quotes it as "the maiden," meaning the same thing. Here, then, in Isaiah 7:14, is a clear statement of the virgin birth of Christ. But that is not all! The same verse plainly says that the Son born of this virgin would be "Immanuel," literally "God with us." That verse in Isaiah claimed that Jesus is God.

Isaiah 9:6 says about the coming Messiah, "For unto us a child is born, unto us a son is given: and the government shall be upon his shoulder: and his name shall be called Wonderful, Counsellor, The mighty God, The everlasting Father, The Prince of Peace." And the following verse clearly foretells that this child will increase in government and eventually will reign forever. And the names of this child are really names of deity. One of His names is "The mighty God." Another of His names is "The everlasting Father." The child to be born, the Son to be given, was to be very God, as clearly deity as God the Father Himself, and in fact a very manifestation of God the Father! And about all these Scriptures Jesus said that anyone who is even slow in heart to believe all the prophets have spoken is a fool (Luke 24:25). Jesus said about such verses that "the scripture cannot be broken" (John 10:35). About these Scriptures and others Jesus said that they are "every word that proceedeth out of the mouth of God" (Luke 4:4; Matt. 4:4). Jesus believed the Old Testament Scriptures that pronounced His own deity.

Second, Jesus clearly declared His own virgin birth.

When Mary His mother said to Him, "Son, why hast thou thus dealt with us? behold, thy father and I have sought thee sorrowing," Jesus answered her, "Wist ye not that I must be about my Father's business?" (Luke 2:48, 49). But Joseph, who sought the twelve-year-old Jesus, was not His father! Rather, staying at the temple, He was about His Father's business. There is no mistaking the meaning of Jesus. Joseph was not His father. but He was born of a virgin, miraculously conceived, God in human form. The Pharisees, shamefully hinting that Jesus was the illegitimate child of Joseph and Mary, said to Jesus, "We be not born of fornication; we have one Father, even God" (John 8:41). Can you see the sneers on their faces as they said it? Here is Jesus' answer: "If God were your Father, ye would love me: for I proceeded forth and came from God; neither came I of myself, but he sent me" (John 8:42). Remember that the question under discussion is whether or not Jesus was born of fornication. His physical birth is the subject, and Jesus said plainly that He proceeded forth and came from God in a sense that could not be true about these Pharisees. Jesus referred to His virgin birth, clearly.

Jesus repeatedly referred to Himself as God's "only begotten Son." Now the word "begat" is a word of human genealogies, a term referring to the male part in procreating or generating a child. It refers to the physical birth. Jesus insisted that He was not begotten of Joseph but was begotten of God. The same word, *monogenes*, is used six times in the New Testament about Jesus as the only-begotten of God, and twice Jesus Himself used it about Himself! Note that Jesus does not claim to be simply one who is begotten of God. Rather, He claims to be the only one ever born who was so begotten. He is the *only* begotten Son of God. No one else was ever born of a virgin. In a spiritual sense, it may be said that Christians are "begotten . . . again unto a lively hope" (I Pet. 1: 3), but in the sense in which Jesus was begotten of God, no one else ever was. Clearly Jesus was claiming that He was physically begotten of God and not by any human father.

Third, Jesus boldly affirmed His deity. That is what Jesus meant when He claimed to be in a peculiar sense the Son of God. It is a modern idea—not even hinted at in the Bible, and never believed by any large number of Christians anywhere—that Jesus could be the Son of God as He claimed to be without actually being deity, the God-man. John the Baptist declared that the Lord Jesus Christ, even while He was on earth, was still "in the bosom of the Father" (John 1: 18); and Jesus told Nicodemus exactly the same thing, that He was "even the Son of man which is in heaven" (John 3: 13). John the Baptist declared that Jesus was "in the beginning with God," that "all things were made by him; and without him was not any thing made that was made," that "in him was life; and the life was the light of men" (John 1: 1-4). That is a clear claim that Christ is deity. Did Jesus teach the same thing? He certainly did. In John 4: 14 He clearly states that He is the author of everlasting life. In John 5: 17 Jesus plainly said, "My Father worketh hitherto, and I work." Did He mean that God was His Father in the sense that other men might say the same thing? Certainly not! He meant that He Himself was one with God. And that is exactly what the Pharisees and all His hearers understood Him to mean, for the next verse says, "Therefore the Jews sought the more to kill him, because he not only had broken the sabbath, but said also that God was his Father, *making himself equal with God*" (John 5: 17, 18). Every honest man who reads the statements of Jesus must know that He claimed to be "equal with God." That is what He meant when He called God His Father and Himself the only begotten Son of God.

In John 5: 20 Jesus claimed knowledge equal with the Father. He said, "For the Father loveth the Son, and sheweth him all things that himself doeth." In verse 21 He claims power equal with the Father, saying, "For as the Father raiseth up the dead, and quickeneth them; even so the Son quickeneth whom he will." That is as strong a claim of deity as Jesus could make.

Jesus claimed honor equal with the Father. In John 5: 22, 23, He says that the Father "hath committed all judgment unto the Son: That all men should honour the Son, even as they honour the Father. He that honoureth not the Son honoureth not the Father which hath sent him." That is a claim of deity.

In that same chapter, verses 25 and 26, Jesus claims that He Himself is the author of life, exactly as the Father in Heaven is. "Verily, verily, I say unto you, The hour is coming, and now is, when the dead shall hear the voice of the Son of God: and they that hear shall live. For as the Father hath life in himself; so hath he given to the Son to have life in himself." Jesus had life in Himself in the same sense that the Father has life in Himself. Jesus is the author of life in exactly the same sense that God the Father is the author of life. Jesus does the works of God, has the power of God, has the knowledge of God, has the honor of God. So He Himself declared. This is "the religion of Jesus." This is "the message of Jesus." Those who do not believe in Christ's deity do not believe in His spirit, His message, His religion.

In John 6: 33, 35 Jesus plainly says that He is the bread come down from Heaven.

In John 6: 46 Jesus plainly says that He alone of all men was of God in a peculiar sense.

In John 8: 19 Jesus claimed identity with the Father. "If ye had known me, ye should have known my Father also." Referring to His claim of deity as being one with the Father, God incarnate, Jesus said to the Pharisees, "If ye believe not that I am he, ye shall die in your sins" (John 8: 24).

Here is the very center and foundation of the religion of Jesus. He is God come in human form. One who does not believe that Christ is what He claimed to be— the virgin-born, only begotten Son of God—must die in his sins, a poor doomed soul! So Jesus Himself taught.

In fact Jesus Himself claimed the very name of deity. When Moses asked God what was His name, he was instructed to tell the children of Israel, "I AM hath sent me unto you" (Exod. 3: 14). Referring to that name of the Father, Jesus said in John 8: 58, "Verily, verily, I say unto you, Before Abraham was, I am." He was the eternal Word, the Creator, the *I Am* of the Old Testament. Jesus could make no stronger claim to deity than that. In John 10: 28 Jesus claims to give eternal life, claims that no one can ever take one of His sheep out of His hand, and then says, "My Father, which gave them me, is greater than all; and no man is able to pluck them out of my Father's hand. I and my Father are one" (John 10: 29, 30). The Jews understood that Jesus was claiming deity for Himself, because they took up stones to stone Him, "because that thou, being a man, makest thyself God" (vs. 33). All who read what Jesus said, if they be open-minded, must also see that He *"makest thyself God"!*

Jesus claimed His deity in Matthew 19: 17. When a rich young ruler called Jesus, "Good Master," or "Rabbi," Jesus said unto him, "Why callest thou me good? there is none good but one, that is, God." Jesus did not say that He was not good. Never once in any word in any Gospel did Jesus ever hint that He was a sinner. No one ever successfully accused Him of sin. No, Jesus plainly said, 'Do not call me good if I am only a rabbi, a teacher. If you call me good, you must admit my deity.' Christ alone, of all men who ever lived on earth, was wholly good, for He was God. Jesus said the same thing again in Mark 10: 18, "Why callest thou me good? there is none good but one, that is, God." Jesus was not willing to be called simply a rabbi, a teacher; that is, a professor or master. He insisted that those who admitted His goodness must admit His deity. And that is sensible. All honest men, sensible men, must take their choice. Either Jesus was not good or He was God. If

He was not what He claimed to be—God in human form —then He was an imposter, a liar, a deceiver.

The testimony of Mark and John joins with that of Matthew and Luke in proclaiming the virgin birth and deity of Christ.

Jesus claimed that He always submitted Himself to the Father, that He had emptied Himself of heavenly glory as Creator to appear in the form of man. But always when He claimed to be the Son of God He meant it was in a peculiar sense such as no other being could ever claim. He claimed to be one with the Father, to have all the power of God, all the wisdom of God, all the personality of God; so that anyone who knew Him would know God. Whatever Jesus said, God said it. Whatever Jesus did, God did it. Whatever Jesus was, God was. So Jesus Himself claimed from the beginning to the end of His ministry.

4. Paul Believed in the Deity and Virgin Birth of Christ

You say, "As to the 'virgin birth,' is it not strange— if belief in it is so necessary for the soul's salvation, as you, I take it, maintain—that Jesus Himself *never mentioned it,* nor do either Paul or the writer of the Gospel of John." I have already shown clearly that the Gospel of John repeatedly refers to Christ as "the only begotten of the Father," or "the only begotten Son," and that Jesus Himself insisted that He was deity, that He was begotten of God in a physical sense, as no other man in the world was ever begotten. You say, "Is it not strange

—." No, what the rest of the Bible says about the deity of Christ and His virgin birth is not at all strange. To me it is surpassingly strange that anybody who claims to be intelligent and who claims to want to teach what Jesus taught and to have His message, His spirit, His religion, should try to deny the deity that is everywhere in the Bible implied and is frequently stated. But let us see what Paul really taught concerning Christ's deity. A few references will be conclusive.

First, Paul claimed that Jesus was risen bodily from the dead, that he himself had seen Him and talked with Him at his conversion on the road to Damascus. Paul described that meeting in Acts 22: 6-10. Again in I Corinthians 15: 3, 4, Paul says that Christ died for our sins as God's atoning sacrifice and Lamb, that He rose from the dead the third day. And then in verse 8, he clearly says that he himself saw the resurrected Christ. That shows that Paul regarded Jesus exactly as all Bible-believers regard Him; as very God, the virgin-born Son of God, miraculously conceived and miraculously raised from the dead. I can see that the personal, bodily resurrection of Christ following His atoning death, as foretold in the Scriptures, involves Christ's deity and the virgin birth taught in the Scriptures. If Paul could not see that, he was not very bright! If you, dear brother, had the viewpoint of Paul, you would never again doubt the very deity of Christ nor question His virgin birth.

Second, Paul believed that Christ was literally "the image of the invisible God," as Colossians 1: 15 declares. The same thing is plainly stated in II Corinthians 4: 4.

And Paul says exactly what the Gospel of John says, that Christ was really the pre-existent Creator of all things. "For by him were all things created, that are in heaven, and that are in earth, visible and invisible, whether they be thrones, or dominions, or principalities, or powers: all things were created by him, and for him: And he is before all things, and by him all things consist" (Col. 1: 16, 17). That statement of Paul, by divine inspiration, is as strong for the deity of Christ as any ever made in the Bible or outside of it. And the claim that Paul—who believed that about Jesus—doubted His virgin birth is either infamous and insincere, or the thoughtless statement of a man who never investigated what Paul said about Christ.

And remember that Paul believed all the Old Testament Scriptures and all the New Testament Scriptures. He said, "All scripture is given by inspiration of God" (II Tim. 3: 16). Paul really had "the religion of Jesus." He really believed and preached "the message of Jesus." And since Paul believed the Scriptures, as Jesus did, it was no trouble for him to believe the virgin birth so clearly foretold in Isaiah 7: 14 and in the incarnation of deity explicitly declared in Isaiah 9: 6. Paul believed exactly what his friend and companion for years, Luke the beloved physician, believed. Paul and Luke never differed a particle on the virgin birth of Christ.

He is no honest scholar who makes Paul and Jesus contradict one another. Great believing Bible scholars of historic Christianity through the centuries have believed that the Gospels and the Epistles all agree to this.

5. The Bible Foretells the Rise of Wicked Men Who Would Deny the Deity of Christ, Pervert the Scriptures, and Do It for Evil Motives

Here are some Scriptures that every modernist, every man who denies the deity, the virgin birth, the substitutionary and atoning death of Christ, should take to heart. The coming of this wicked unbelief is foretold in the Bible. We are clearly told that it is of Satan. We are told that those who deny the Bible doctrine of Christ are insincere, that they have evil motives, that they use feigned and deceitful words and that they do it to make merchandise of men. Consider the following Scriptures:

"Beloved, when I gave all diligence to write unto you of the common salvation, it was needful for me to write unto you, and exhort you that ye should earnestly contend for the faith which was once delivered unto the saints. For there are certain men crept in unawares, who were before of old ordained to this condemnation, ungodly men, turning the grace of our God into lasciviousness, and denying the only Lord God, and our Lord Jesus Christ."—Jude 3, 4.

First Timothy 4: 1, 2 says,

"Now the Spirit speaketh expressly, that in the latter times some shall depart from the faith, giving heed to seducing spirits, and doctrines of devils; Speaking lies in hypocrisy; having their conscience seared with a hot iron."

Second Peter 2: 1-3 says,

"But there were false prophets also among the people,

*even as there shall be false teachers among you, who
privily shall bring in damnable heresies, even denying the
Lord that bought them and bring upon themselves swift
destruction.   And many shall follow their pernicious
ways; by reason of whom the way of truth shall be evil
spoken of.   And through covetousness shall they with
feigned words make merchandise of you: whose judgment now of a long time lingereth not, and their damnation slumbereth not."*

You see that it was clearly foretold that false teachers
should "privily . . . bring in damnable heresies, even
denying the Lord that bought them"; that these modernists "through covetousness shall . . . with feigned words
make merchandise of you."   And we are clearly told
that terrible judgments will come on such unbelievers in
the Lord Jesus.

Second John 7 says,

*"For many deceivers are entered into the world, who
confess not that Jesus Christ is come in the flesh.   This
is a deceiver and an antichrist."*

Remember that the word *Christ* refers always to the
Old Testament Messiah, the One so long foretold in
prophecy; Immanuel, the mighty God, the One born of a
virgin, the Lamb of God.   One who does not believe that
the pre-existent Christ, one with the Father, has come
in the flesh is a deceiver and antichrist, the Scripture
says.

And what shall real Christians, Bible-believing Christians, Christians who have the message and the spirit and
the religion of Jesus Christ—what shall they do about

such modernism? The same second epistle of John tells us, in verses 9 to 11, what we are to do:

"Whosoever transgresseth, and abideth not in the doctrine of Christ, hath not God. He that abideth in the doctrine of Christ, he hath both the Father and the Son. If there come any unto you, and bring not this doctrine, receive him not into your house, neither bid him God speed: For he that biddeth him God speed is partaker of his evil deeds"!

One who is wrong in the Bible doctrine of Christ, including His deity, His virgin birth, His miracles, His bodily resurrection, His atoning blood—such a one "hath not God." He is not saved, is not a Christian, is not going to Heaven. And Christian people are not to receive such a modernist into their houses and are not to bid him God speed, lest they be partakers of his evil deeds!

Oh, beware of the deadly sin of modernism!

Again, friend, I ask you to forgive my delay. I wanted to give a carefully prepared and adequate answer to your questions. If they were sincere questions, as I trust they were, then you will take to heart this Bible answer and will set out really to follow the faith of Jesus, to have the religion of Jesus and promote His message. That will involve the acceptance of the Bible as the infallible Word of God, the acceptance of Christ as God's own Son in a peculiar way as declared in the Bible, which involves His virgin birth, His pre-existence as God, as the very Creator, and involves His atoning death as God's sacrifice for sin and the only Saviour. May God open your heart and your mind to see the light, and may you have courage and integrity enough to leave your sins, your pride and prejudices, and to come to Jesus, who Himself is the Light and the only Way to God and the only Way to Heaven!

With earnest love and prayers, yours,

John R. Rice

Chapter 2

LETTER TO A MODERNIST

In *The Sword of the Lord* some months ago was printed a letter which I wrote to a modernist in New York City who had attended our tent revival campaign in Brooklyn and who had written to me denying the deity of Christ and the authority of the Bible, though he claimed to be Christian and thought we should preach, he said, "the message of Jesus."

My letter to him was published under the title, "Is Jesus God?" Later I received his answer protesting that it was uncivil to class him with infidels and not to call him a Christian brother. He made the charge that these infidels in the church often make against us who believe the Bible and accept Jesus Christ as deity, as the virgin-born Son of God, as God's atoning Saviour for sinners. He said that we Bible Christians are intolerant and uncivil in not accepting modernists as Christian brothers. Here is my answer to his letter, very carefully written.

Dear Mr. J——:

Your letter of October 15 is before me, and I have very prayerfully considered what you have to say.

You say that "viewed on the plane of human civility," my last letter to you deserves no reply.

But why, Mr. J——, should this battle between Chris-

tianity and anti-Christianity be on the mere plane of
human civility? Why should the friends of Jesus Christ,
those who love Him, who trust Him, who accept Him
as exactly what He claimed to be—the very Son of God,
deity incarnate in human flesh—why should we be so
politely civil to those who would take the crown of deity
from the head of the Son of God? Why maintain such
an anxiety for politeness? Why strive so hard not to
offend the enemies of the cross of Christ? Must we
Christians be more civil than our Saviour?

How Civil Were Jesus and the Apostles, Paul and John, to Religious Infidels?

I wrote you in the language of the Lord Jesus Himself, quoting His words in Matthew 23 to others, like
yourself, very religious in observance, but denying
Christ's deity, rejecting Him as Saviour, as you do.

The religious leaders in the days of Christ professed
to worship the true God, as you do. They professed the
best in scholarship, as you do. They professed to follow
the spirit of the Bible, as you do. Yet they rejected
Christ, they denied His deity, they believed He was an
illegitimate child of Joseph, not the virgin-born Son of
God, just as you believe the same. They would not admit His deity; they would not accept Him as Saviour.
Neither do you. And to these, Jesus said seven times,
"Woe unto you, scribes and Pharisees, hypocrites!" Jesus said that they were whited sepulchres, outwardly very
nice, inwardly rotten.

He said they were blind leaders of the blind. He said,
"Ye serpents, ye generation of vipers, how can ye
escape the damnation of hell?" If that is the way Jesus
Christ described those religious leaders who denied His
claims while pretending to serve God, why should not
all true Christians feel just as Jesus did feel then and
does feel now about it? And you talk about "human
civility!"

In I Corinthians 16: 22 the Apostle Paul, by inspiration, said, "If any man love not the Lord Jesus Christ,
let him be Anathema Maran-atha." And the word for
love here means *be a friend of.* No one is a friend of
the Lord Jesus Christ who denies that He is Lord, who
denies He is the pre-existent Christ, who denies He is
what He claims to be, and would make Him an illegitimate human child, an imposter, claiming what
He was not. And Paul connected this anathema with
the second coming of the Lord Jesus Christ, as the word
maranatha in the Aramaic plainly shows. Those who do
not believe that Jesus is Christ, that He is Lord, that
He is coming again, are accursed. So said Paul. So
say I and others who believe the Bible and love the Lord
Jesus Christ. Why should I be more civil than Paul?
When divine inspiration in the Bible puts a curse on
unbelievers in Christ, who am I to contradict divine
inspiration?

Let me add here a Scripture. In Galatians 1: 7-9 Paul,
by divine inspiration, says:

"*. . . there be some that trouble you, and would pervert the gospel of Christ. But though we, or an angel
from heaven, preach any other gospel unto you than that*

*which we have preached unto you, let him be accursed.
As we said before, so say I now again, If any man preach
any other gospel unto you than that ye have received, let
him be accursed."*

Any modernist who brings any gospel besides the gospel of individual salvation by personal faith in the blood
of Christ should be accursed, and Paul repeated it: "Let
him be accursed"! Paul was not 'civil' to these religious
hypocrites pretending to be Christians.

In II John 9, 10 we are plainly told that you modernists who transgress and do not abide in the doctrine of
Christ, do not have God. And we are plainly commanded, "If there come any unto you, and bring not this
doctrine, receive him not into your house, neither bid
him God speed: For he that biddeth him God speed is
partaker of his evil deeds." Instead of dealing with infidels and modernists (who deny the Bible and deny the
deity of Christ and forsake the historic position of Bible
Christianity) on the mere shallow plane of human civility, why not deal with them on the Bible basis, the basis
commanded by our God and our Saviour?

If I would not call Bob Ingersoll a Christian, why
should I call you a Christian, who promulgate the same
Christ-denying infidelity? The difference is that Bob
Ingersoll was honest in that he never pretended to be a
Christian. You modernists, however, take holy vows to
be true to the gospel, to historic creeds that represent the
Christendom of the centuries and represent the main
fundamentals of the Bible. Modernist infidels differ
from apostates and infidels of other days only in that
they are dishonest, pretending to be Christian in order

to have the respectability and the salaries and positions provided by Christians. So the unbeliever in the church is not even to be received into the home of a Christian, is not even to have the greeting, "God speed." I confess that I seek no friendship of hypocrites who pretend to love the Lord Jesus, pretend to be Christians, and then deny every fundamental of the Christian faith, and stab Christ in the back and try to wreck the faith of the young and innocent and the ignorant. I say frankly that I am trying to be true to Christ; I am not specially striving for what you call "human civility." If I talk as the Lord Jesus Christ talked about His detractors and deniers, it will not appear polite. If I pronounce the anathema that Paul pronounced on those untrue to Christ, I will not appear civil. If I follow the plain instructions (inspired of God) of the beloved Apostle John, I will not please infidels in the church, who want the friendship and the money of honest Christians while they deny the deity of Jesus Christ.

From Jesus Back to Paul!

In your first two letters you were insisting that I should have "the spirit of Jesus," that I should preach "the message of Jesus." And now I have called to your attention the fact that Jesus insisted, concerning the Bible, that "every word . . . proceedeth out of the mouth of God" (Matt. 4: 4), and that Jesus insisted that every jot and tittle of even the Old Testament were inspired of God and would never pass away (Matt. 5: 17, 18); that Jesus insisted that only those born again could ever, by supernatural regeneration, by faith in Christ as God's atoning Lamb, enter Heaven (John 3:1-18), and pronounced terrible woes on all who denied His deity. So now you leave off talking about "the spirit of Jesus" and "the message of Jesus" and return to the Paul you formerly despised! Now you want me to be like Paul. How strange you modernists are, to quote a Bible that you do not believe, to hold up a fundamentalist like Paul as an example when you yourself would do anything on earth before you would take Paul as your pattern, as a gospel preacher! So you want us to have the attitude of Paul toward the gospel and toward Christ? That is exactly what all Bible believers want to do! And let us see where that brings us.

Modernists Want 'The Spirit, Not the Letter,' as Paul Did, They Say

You say, "I feel you would do well to heed the example of Paul as to his presentation of the gospel as declared in his statement: '. . . but our sufficiency is of God; Who also hath made us able ministers of the new testament; *not of the letter, but of the spirit: for the letter killeth, but the spirit giveth life'* " (II Cor. 3:5,6).

I note that you want us to take the example of Paul. And in the following paragraph you say, ". . . . I feel pity for you, who have shackled your God-given reason and good judgment by becoming a slave to the letter of the written human record of God's revelation through His Son Jesus Christ and are insensible to the spirit of this revelation and the progressive unfolding of it through the centuries by the Holy Spirit's enlightenment of consecrated human hearts and intelligences to meet changing thought and needs."

Several things ought to be said about these statements of yours.

First, they are manifestly insincere. No modernist denying the deity of Christ, denying the integrity and accuracy of the Bible, really follows "the example of Paul as to his presentation of the gospel." And this insincerity is further manifested when you speak of Jesus as "His Son Jesus Christ," when you have repeatedly, in former letters, denied Christ's deity, denied the virgin birth, denied His atoning death on the cross. All modernists pervert Bible language for their own insincere uses. Harry Emerson Fosdick says in his book, *The Hope of the World,* in the sermon, "The Peril of Worshipping Jesus," that of course Jesus is divine, even as Fosdick's mother was divine. That is a deliberately dishonest use of the word divine, making it mean humanity instead of deity. And you who have already said that Jesus is not deity, and is not the Son of God in the sense that He claimed to be, having been pre-existent with the Father, really being one of the triune God, now talk about Him as being God's Son. You use the language of Christianity with the meaning of an infidel, and that is criminally dishonest.

Note that on the matter of the inspiration of the Bible, you insist that we follow the example of Paul. You would have us believe that Paul did not believe in the letter of the Scriptures, did not believe in the absolute authenticity and accuracy and infallibility of the Scriptures. You would have us believe that Paul had the spirit of present-day modernists. Shame on you! If you really do not know what was Paul's stand and attitude concerning the inspiration of the Scriptures, how naive you are! And if you do know, and insincerely try to pretend that Paul did not believe in the very letter of the Bible as being absolutely inspired of God and supernaturally infallible in the original manuscripts, then oh, what hypocrisy!

In I Corinthians 2: 9-14 Paul gives us a clear doctrine of the inspiration of the Bible, the same doctrine that is taught in both the Old and the New Testaments. The doctrine is summed up in I Corinthians 2: 13: "Which things also we speak, not in words which man's wisdom teacheth, but which the Spirit teacheth: combining spiritual things with spiritual words" (R.V.).

Paul says that the matter of his teaching was all revealed by the Holy Spirit and that likewise the very words were given by the Holy Spirit. And then Paul answers all this folly about men thinking out and understanding God and being able to judge the Bible. Paul says in the next verse, "But the natural man receiveth not the things of the Spirit of God: for they are foolishness unto him: neither can he know them, because they are spiritually discerned." And when Paul uses the word "spiritually" he means that they are discerned by the Holy Spirit, not by human wisdom. The only way we have to know the things of God is as they are revealed by the Holy Spirit to converted men who accept the divine revelation in the Bible. Paul's doctrine was that God gave the very words of the Bible. It is childish and wicked to pretend that you have the attitude of Paul, "as to his presentation of the gospel" when you deny that the Bible is a reliable, supernaturally infallible revelation from God. Paul insists that the very words were inspired of God, as well as the thoughts. Paul says that his teaching (which is now incorporated in our New Testament) was that which the Holy Ghost taught him, teaching Spirit-given matters with Spirit-given, New Testament words. How can you deny inspiration of the Scriptures and pretend that you follow the example of Paul?

What Paul Meant by Contrast of Letter and Spirit

When Paul said that he was an able minister of the New Testament, "not of the letter, but of the spirit: for the letter killeth, but the spirit giveth life," in II Corinthians 3: 6, what did he mean? It is certain that he did not mean to contradict what he so plainly stated in I Corinthians about the inspiration of even the words of Scripture in the original manuscripts. He did not mean to contradict what Jesus Himself had said about even the jots and tittles being inspired of God, and that every word of the Scripture proceeded from the mouth of God. Paul certainly was not taking the modernists' position, denying the inspiration of the Bible, which doctrine he had so valiantly taught heretofore.

But we have to read the context to see exactly what Paul meant. Immediately following the statement that "the letter killeth, but the spirit giveth life," verses 7 to 11 continue, as follows:

"But if the ministration of death, written and engraven in stones, was glorious, so that the children of Israel could not stedfastly behold the face of Moses for the glory of his countenance; which glory was to be done away: How shall not the ministration of the spirit be rather glorious? For if the ministration of condemnation be glory, much more doth the ministration of righteousness exceed in glory. For even that which was made glorious had no glory in this respect, by reason of the glory that excelleth. For if that which is done away was glorious, much more that which remaineth is glorious."

It is clear here that Paul is saying he is not a minister of the Mosaic law "written and engraven in stones," the old covenant with Israel, which was as a schoolmaster to bring them to Christ. That indeed was glorious, says Paul by divine inspiration, and how much more is the gospel that Paul preaches of salvation by the blood of Christ! The law never saved anybody. It was "the ministration of condemnation" (vs. 9). No one was ever truly righteous according to the law of the Old Testament, for "all have sinned, and come short of the glory of God," as Paul elsewhere says by inspiration.

Yet that Old Testament law was inspired of God and had a rich spiritual meaning. In fact, the spiritual meaning of the Old Testament ceremonial law is the same as the New Testament gospel. For example, Paul did not preach that Jews must observe the Passover with the slain lamb and the blood on the door. Rather, he preached that that lamb typified Christ. The lamb was

without blemish, and Christ was without sin. The blood
of the lamb on the door of an Israelite in Egypt pictured
the fact that a sinner can have all his sins covered by
the blood of Jesus Christ. That lamb roasted with fire
and eaten with bitter herbs pictures the infinite sufferings of Christ for man's sins. And the spiritual applica-
tion of the Old Testament ceremonial law is what Paul
preached in his gospel.

Paul did not preach that Jews must be circumcised in
the flesh. Rather, he taught that circumcision was a
type of the new birth, and that sinners need to be circumcised in heart, born again, receiving a new nature
from God when they trust Christ for salvation. Paul
preached the spiritual meaning of circumcision.

Paul did not preach the letter of ceremonial law, that
one must observe Saturday, the Jewish Sabbath, the
seventh day of the week, as a day of rest. Rather, he
taught that as Christ rose the first day of the week, so
a Christian can, in the very beginning of his life, have
sweet rest and peace with God and then live out his days
already saved, and find a Sabbath of rest awaiting in
Heaven. Paul did not preach the letter of ceremonial
law. He preached the spiritual lessons which are inherent in the ceremonies of the law, and preached the
righteousness of the law fulfilled in Christ. That is
made clear in Romans 10: 1-13, and in many other places
in Paul's writing.

Paul plainly taught that the Old Testament Scriptures
were inspired of God and infallibly correct, but that
the true meaning of even the Old Testament Scriptures
was not salvation by circumcision, not salvation by ani-

mal sacrifices, not salvation by keeping the Ten Commandments, but rather that salvation came by faith
in the Lamb of God, God's own Son who should die
for man's sin.

Pharisees and scribes taught the letter of the Old Testament without understanding its spiritual meaning
at all. Paul plainly said that he was not like them.
Only as one opens his heart so that the Spirit of God
may reveal Christ in the Old Testament teachings can
he get the real meaning, and that is what Paul is preaching here.

We should never try to define Paul's gospel except as
he himself so definitely defined it in I Corinthians 15,
verses 1 to 4:

*"Moreover, brethren, I declare unto you the gospel
which I preached unto you, which also ye have received,
and wherein ye stand; By which also ye are saved, if
ye keep in memory what I preached unto you, unless ye
have believed in vain. For I delivered unto you first of
all that which I also received, how that Christ died for
our sins according to the scriptures; And that he was
buried, and that he rose again the third day according to
the scriptures."*

Note the following facts about this Scripture:

1. This is the gospel Paul preached, the one that the
people at Corinth received, and the one they believed
and by which they were saved.

2. This is the gospel Paul had received from God
(vs. 3).

3. The gospel was threefold: (a). "That Christ died

for our sins." There is the atoning death of Christ, substitution, salvation by blood. (b). "And that he was buried, and that he rose again the third day." The supernatural, bodily resurrection from the dead was part of Paul's gospel that he preached everywhere and that all Bible Christians received and by which they were saved. (c). That this death and this resurrection were "according to the scriptures" is explicitly stated twice in this passage which defines Paul's gospel. Paul's gospel was always "according to the scriptures," and the very word Scriptures means what is written down, the divine writings of the Old Testament, supernaturally inspired.

When you speak of Paul's gospel and do not mean this, then it is either ignorance or hypocrisy.

It is true that Paul preached according to the Spirit, not merely according to the letter of Old Testament ceremonial law. But Paul did not anywhere cast reflection on the integrity of the letter of Scriptures. Everywhere Paul insists that the Scriptures were inspired of God, as he expressly says in II Timothy 3: 16.

How can Bible believers respect either the scholarship or the integrity of modernists, when they either have not studied or they intentionally pervert these most simple fundamental teachings of the New Testament, clearly understood for centuries by Bible-believing Christians? It is a sad truth, often demonstrated, that modernists are not scholarly as regards the Bible, and that they are not honest when they use Bible terms. When a modernist uses the word "gospel," he does not mean what the Bible means by the term. "Inspiration," "divinity," and "salvation" are terms deliberately perverted by modernists.

Are Bible-believing Christians "Slaves to the Letter" of the Bible?

You say, "I feel pity for you, who have shackled your God-given reason and good judgment by becoming a slave to the letter of the written human record of God's revelation." Again you say, "It is indeed sad that the fulfillment of Christ's purpose in the advance of the reign of God among men is thus retarded by such slaves to the letter as you."

How familiar your language is! That is the way Satan has always talked to people about turning to God, about turning to Christ for salvation, and surrendering to Him as Lord.

How many young couples, some of whom I have known personally, have boasted that they were "no longer enslaved" by authority when they lived together in shameful adultery, unmarried! Now they were free!

How many young men, living a life of drunkenness and lewdness and gambling, have boasted to me of their freedom! "I would hate to be tied to my mother's apron strings like you are," they said. Or, "To be a Christian, you would have to give up all your liberty and be a slave to rules."

How many lost sinners, thousands of them, in fact, have told me, as I pleaded with them to accept Christ as Saviour, "No, I want to be free. I want to have a good time. I don't want to give up all my rights. I don't want to be bound down by having to live like a Christian."

Yes, your foolish talk about being enslaved by believing the Bible is very familiar to all who have met the wiles of Satan before. And of course it is not strange that you thus talk as profligates and sinners and infidels talk, because your fight is against God, just as all drunkards and harlots and atheists fight against God. They feel about the Bible just as you do, because they are not willing to surrender to Jesus Christ as God's own Son, just as you are not willing to accept Him as Saviour and Lord.

How often modernists and atheists have said that Bible believers were guilty of "bibliolatry" or worship of the Bible. Modernists say that, and so do atheists. In fact, it is a favorite argument of the communistic atheists. They teach as you do—or rather, you teach as they do, for atheists started the argument—that 'religion is the opiate of the people.' Atheists in Russia have boasted that communism will set people free from government bondage and will also free them from the bondage of Bible Christianity. Russian communistic cartoons show communism climbing up a ladder to Heaven to hit God the Father and the Holy Spirit and God the Son over the head with the Russian hammer. They speak of the bondage of the Czars and in the same breath the bondage of the Bible. I say there is a familiar ring to your talk about my being in bondage to the Bible when I believe it.

In fact, that is the argument Satan used in the Garden of Eden with Adam and Eve. God was not fair to them, Satan implied, to keep them in ignorance, bound by rules. Why, if they would only eat of the forbidden fruit, they would be wise like God, knowing good and evil. The

Word of God, forbidding certain sins, is pictured as a hateful bondage that men should break. And you modernists take up this old lie of Satan, and then you expect people still to believe that you love God, that you want to do right, and that you are honest in your rejection of Christ as God in human form, and you expect to be counted as Christians!

How contrary to all the teachings of Jesus, all the teachings of Paul, all the teachings everywhere recorded in the Bible, is your foolish charge! Not once, in all the references to sin in the Bible, is anybody ever charged with the sin of "bibliolatry," the worship of the Bible or Scriptures. Not once did Jesus condemn anybody for believing the Bible and accepting it word for word as the infallible Word of God. Not once anywhere, in either the Old or the New Testament, is there a hint that anybody was either unwise or wrong to accept all of the Scriptures as the very infallible Word of God.

You demand to be free from the letter of the Scriptures, but actually what you think is freedom is bondage. How could there be any freedom when you are enslaved to your own will, enslaved to the opinions of men—poor, human, fallible creatures like yourself? No, the Lord Jesus taught that the only true freedom is under divine authority, the authority of God in Christ and in the divinely inspired Bible. Jesus said in John 8: 31, 32, "If ye continue in my word, then are ye my disciples indeed; And ye shall know the truth, and the truth shall make you free." People are not made free by going without authority, without some center of doctrine, without some written form of truth. Only as people follow the words of Jesus are they His disciples, and they can know the truth and the truth will make them free.

And what is the truth that makes men free? Jesus Himself tells us. In that holy prayer in John 17: 17, Jesus said, praying for His disciples, "Sanctify them through thy truth: thy word is truth." Oh, the prayer of the Lord Jesus is that men may be sanctified by the written Word of God which is the truth.

And Jesus said the truth, the truth in the Bible, makes men free.

Modernists are not free. They are slaves of their own passion, their own pride. They are slaves of the changing winds of public opinions. They cannot save themselves and they cannot save others. They do not have any remedy for the drunkard enslaved by his habit, the whoremonger enslaved by his passion. They have no remedy for anybody enslaved by sin.

Paul was glad to call himself the bondslave of Jesus Christ, but oh, the glad freedom of Paul in his beloved bondage! And all who have really come to Christ in absolute surrender and trust have found what the Bible calls "the liberty wherewith Christ hath made us free" (Gal. 5: 1).

Now when people know the truth of the Bible and believe it and follow it, "the truth shall make you free," said Jesus; and He said, "Thy word is truth."

Anarchists want liberty without law, in human government.

Modernists want liberty without the authority of God's Word.

There is a definite kinship in the two.

Does Believing the Bible Retard God's Cause?

You say, "It is indeed sad that the fulfillment of Christ's purpose in the advance of the reign of God among men is thus retarded by such slaves to the letter as you." Now what do you mean by "the fulfillment of Christ's purpose"? He plainly told us, "The Son of man is come to seek and to save that which was lost" (Luke 19:10). And I Timothy 1:15 tells us, "This is a faithful saying, and worthy of all acceptation, that Christ Jesus came into the world to save sinners; of whom I am chief." The purpose of Christ is to save sinners, to get people converted, keeping them from Hell and winning them to Heaven.

In the words of John 3:16, we see that God the Father and Christ the Son have had the same purpose from the beginning; God so loved and Christ so suffered, "that whosoever believeth in him should not perish, but have everlasting life." What else could be the fulfillment of Christ's purpose, the advance of the reign of God, except getting individuals saved, born again? And do you really claim that modernists do that?

According to your poor theory, then, D. L. Moody, who believed all the Bible as the very Word of God—just as I do—was a great hindrance to the cause of Christ. He won only about a million souls! And Charles Spurgeon and John Wesley and Charles G. Finney and R. A. Torrey and many others who have won their multitudes to trust in Jesus Christ, were hinderers of the fulfillment of Christ's purpose, you say! Under their preaching drunkards were made sober, the immoral were made pure, wrecked homes were reunited. Criminals, enemies of society, were made into good citizens. The revival under Wesley saved England from a second French Revolution, as the best historians agree. And you think his kind of gospel hinders the cause of Christ! D. L. Moody, with his fervent preaching of the blood of Christ as the only hope for man's sin—believing just what I believe—profoundly affected for good the morals of America more than any other man who ever lived. And you say that Bible believers hinder the purpose of Christ!

In my poor ministry I have seen tens of thousands publicly claim Christ as Saviour. Hundreds of them were drunkards who quit their drink. A good number were convicted criminals who, after coming to Christ, went straight and made good citizens. Dozens of them were fallen women who, after coming to Christ, lived transformed, happy, virtuous lives. Homes broken by divorce were reunited when these who came to Christ as Saviour, believing in His deity, believing in His virgin birth, His bodily resurrection, His miracles, as I do, were converted under my preaching.

Evidently you do not know what **is** the purpose of Christ, what **is** "the fulfillment of Christ's purpose."

When have modernists held any great revivals? The Federal Council of Churches has sent preaching missions all over America, and not once have they resulted in a great revival, a great turning to God. Modernists cannot have a revival. When you do not believe the Bible, when you do not accept Christ as the virgin-born, pre-existent Creator that He claimed to be, you have nothing to produce a revival. You have no gospel that can change hearts or help men.

Modernists have had a wonderful chance in Germany. Remember that the German colleges and seminaries were the first to go over en masse to the position of you modernists. Out of that rejection of the Bible came the flowering of the doctrine of Karl Marx and of Nietzsche. Out of it came the German teaching that "might makes right." Out of that came the First World War and out of it likewise has come the Second World War. Hitler himself was the flowering of modernism. If all of us came from brute beasts, if the Bible is not true, if sin is only relative, if there is no Hell, no judgment; then, says German higher criticism (what we call modernism), why should not men take by force whatever they want? Only modernism, breaking down the faith of German people, made possible Hitler's rise to power. Hitler's doctrine is the doctrine of modernism. Hitler and his Nazi party typified the modernists. Do you really believe that these have aided in the fulfilling of the purpose of Christ in the world? Certainly you cannot say that Hitler and the Nazi party in Germany were slaves to the letter of the Bible! No, they have been "emancipated" by the same doctrine that you modernists teach in America.

The communists in Russia agree with you perfectly when you say you do not believe in the accuracy of the Bible, do not accept the deity of Christ, do not accept His virgin birth, His bodily resurrection, nor acknowledge any need for His atoning blood. Certainly the communists have been set free from what you call slavery. Stalin is certainly no "slave to the letter of the written human record." No wonder a large percentage of the modernistic leaders in America are friendly to communism; they have so much in common. Both are enemies of New Testament Christianity, both deny the deity of Christ, both deny the accuracy and authority of the Scriptures. But Russia with her blood-purges, her murder of millions, her millions now in concentration camps, even today, for religious and political (not moral) offenses, is not fulfilling the purpose of Christ, is not bringing in the reign of God. Russians live under slavery more terrible even than Hitler's, yet by your theory they ought to feel the freest in the world, because they are not slaves enough to believe the Bible!

You Admit You Were Not Converted, Even When You Tried to Believe the Bible

You say that "during the many years when I was trying to accept as true the main doctrines which you emphasize as essential to salvation, God was to me a far-off deity." I want to speak gently here, and not to be unkind. But evidently here is your whole trouble. Even when you were trying to believe the Bible, you say that God was a far-off deity. You never were born into His family; you never had the Holy Spirit put it into your heart to say, "Abba, Father." You never claim to have been born into His family. You never knew what it was to repent of your sins, be converted, born again, and so receive everlasting life. God's Holy Spirit did not have a chance to come into your body to live, because you were

never saved. No wonder you did not believe the Bible!
Remember that concerning the very matter of the inspiration of the Bible, Paul says in I Corinthians 2: 13-
15, "Which things also we speak, not in the words which
man's wisdom teacheth, but which the Holy Ghost teacheth; comparing spiritual things with spiritual. But the
natural man receiveth not the things of the Spirit of
God: for they are foolishness unto him: neither can he
know them, because they are spiritually discerned. But
he that is spiritual judgeth all things, yet he himself is
judged of no man." Only as a man comes to confess he is
a poor lost sinner and to trust in Christ for forgiveness
and salvation on the basis of the atoning blood, and so is
made into a new creature, a child of God, can he understand the things of God. Spiritual things are spiritually
discerned, and one who does not have the Spirit of God
within him to teach him, does not understand the things
of God. This Paul emphasizes in the preceding verses,
I Corinthians 2: 9-12. Only the Spirit of God can reveal
the things of God. And He cannot come into your heart
and live in your body, making it His temple, until you
receive Christ as Saviour and by faith are born again,
receiving a new heart, being made a partaker of the divine
nature.

What is wrong with a modernist is that he needs
a new heart. He needs a miracle of regeneration, making him into a child of God. You could believe the Bible
if you were willing to repent of your sins and be converted. Then the Holy Spirit would teach you what you
otherwise can never understand.

But you continue thus: "But now for a number of

years He has most graciously given me a *consciousness of His presence abiding in my life.* If I am a fraud and all your letter names me as being, isn't it strange that God the Father thus gives me the assurance of His presence and guidance in my life?"

No, friend, that does not seem strange to me. A Christian Scientist told me with great eagerness how that Christian Science had met all her need and how she had sweet peace now that she had never had before. Every false religion in the world has its devotees who feel just as you do. Mohammedans scorn Christianity and are perfectly satisfied that they alone have the favor of God. Many Hindus scorn Christianity and tell of the satisfaction they have in the prospect of nirvana. Do you suppose that millions would take long treks to Mecca or the Ganges River, or would offer sacrifices in Buddhist temples, if they did not therefrom gain satisfaction and some assurance of God's favor?

I note that you did *not* say, "I have assurance that I am born again, that my sins are covered by the blood of Christ." I note that you do not tell me of a definite transaction when you were converted and born into God's family. I note that you do not base your contentment on any promise of God's Word. Naturally not, since you do not believe that Word of God. You say you have assurance of God's abiding presence in your life.

So Saul of Tarsus felt, until that day on the road to Damascus when he was struck down by a light brighter than the sun and found himself facing Jesus. He had lived blameless according to the law, he said, and had tried to maintain always a conscience void of offense. Yet up to that moment he was a poor, lost sinner and would have gone to Hell, he himself being witness.

The Pharisee came into the temple to pray, as Jesus tells in Luke, chapter 18, and was very well satisfied with himself. He was pleased with his tithes, with his observance of the law, with his religious ceremony, with his outwardly blameless life. But he was not saved. The poor publican who smote upon his breast and cried, "God be merciful to me a sinner," (or "God be propitiated toward me—accept the offered blood in my behalf") went down to his house justified, rather than the Pharisee who was so well pleased with himself!

And Jesus, in Matthew 7: 21-23, says:

"Not every one that saith unto me, Lord, Lord, shall enter into the kingdom of heaven; but he that doeth the will of my Father which is in heaven. Many will say to me in that day, Lord, Lord, have we not prophesied in thy name? and in thy name have cast out devils? and in thy name done many wonderful works? And then will I profess unto them, I never knew you: depart from me, ye that work iniquity."

Not every one who expects to go to Heaven is going there, but only those that do the will of God the Father about salvation. And this will is that they are to believe on Christ whom He has sent, as Jesus Himself said in John 6: 29. Not those who have prophesied in His name, or even have cast out devils, or have done wonderful works in Christ's name; but only those who have come as He commanded us to come for salvation, will enter Heaven. I beg you, do not be deceived by that sense of self-righteousness which has never come to the blood for cleansing.

I well know that modernists, who have forsaken the faith of their fathers, sometimes retain for one generation the morals they were taught in childhood. I know they often have the appearance of Christianity. They talk pleasantly; they have the outward virtues of gentlemen; they speak so reasonably. Of such Paul said, by divine inspiration, in II Corinthians 11:13-15:

"For such are false apostles, deceitful workers, transforming themselves into the apostles of Christ. And no marvel; for Satan himself is transformed into an angel of light. Therefore it is no great thing if his ministers also be transformed as the ministers of righteousness; whose end shall be according to their works."

Satan would not want his main teachers to appear as drunkards and harlots and murderers. Satan himself never appears with horns and forked tongue and tail and pitchfork. And so, says the Scripture, there are "false apostles, deceitful workers, transforming themselves into the apostles of Christ." Satan himself appears an angel of light and "therefore it is no great thing if his ministers also be transformed as the ministers of righteousness." The Jewish leaders who hated Jesus and had Him crucified were very nice, moral people, religious people, boasting of their righteousness and quite assured that no one was as dear to God as they were. But they were poor, doomed sinners, nevertheless, agents of Satan.

In earnest, loving entreaty I write you, pleading that you do not be deceived as they were, but that you repent of your sins, accept the Christ of the Bible as all He claims to be—the virgin-born Creator, God incarnate, who made atonement for our sins on the cross—and accept the Bible for what Jesus claimed it was, the very revelation from God. And if by faith you put Christ to the test, you will find Him all He claims to be, and your doubts will flee away.

In Jesus' dear name, yours,

(Signed) JOHN R. RICE.

Chapter 3

THE VIRGIN-BORN SAVIOUR

"Therefore the Lord himself shall give you a sign; Behold, a virgin shall conceive, and bear a son, and shall call his name Immanuel."—Isa. 7: 14.

"Now the birth of Jesus Christ was on this wise: When as his mother Mary was espoused to Joseph, before they came together, she was found with child of the Holy Ghost."—Matt. 1: 18.

"Then said Mary unto the angel, How shall this be, seeing I know not a man? And the angel answered and said unto her, The Holy Ghost shall come upon thee, and the power of the Highest shall overshadow thee: therefore also that holy thing which shall be born of thee shall be called the Son of God."—Luke 1: 34, 35.

The Scriptures teach that the Lord Jesus was born with a human mother but born without a human father. Mary was a virgin when Christ was conceived and was still a virgin when He was born. She was "with child of the Holy Ghost." The Holy Spirit came upon her and she conceived the holy child Jesus. This is a blessed and vital teaching of the Bible.

Jesus was born of a woman so that He might be "the Son of man." Christmas ought to be a time of rejoicing, a time of praise, a time of devotion. But let us remem-

ber that all the true meaning of Christmas will be forever gone for anyone who throws away his faith in the
virgin birth of our Saviour. If Christ were not virgin-
born, then He is not God. If Christ were not virgin-
born, then He could not be our Saviour. All Christianity stands or falls with the doctrine of the virgin birth.
If Jesus had a human father, then the Bible is not true.
The book of Isaiah is false, the Gospel of Matthew is
false, the Gospel of Luke is false, and the Gospel of John
is false, for all these clearly teach that the Saviour,
the Messiah, was born of a virgin, and was begotten of
God, not begotten of a human father. There is no way
to believe in the inspiration of the Bible if one denies
the Bible claim that Jesus was born of a virgin without
a human father. If Jesus were born of a human father
and the Bible teaching that He was born of a virgin is
untrue, then no sensible man living would believe in His
pre-existence with the Father as taught in the first chapter of John. No sensible person could believe that He is
the Creator of the world, as claimed in Hebrews 1: 2
and Colossians 1: 16, if He be not deity in human form,
begotten of God, miraculously born, a supernatural being. If Jesus be not a supernatural being, God in human flesh, and therefore born of a virgin without a human father, then no sensible person could believe that He
will be the final Judge of all the earth. If Jesus had a
human father and mother just as other men, if He were
not supernaturally, miraculously born, God appearing in
human flesh, then His death on the cross could not atone
for the sins of mankind. All Christianity, I say, stands
or falls with the Bible doctrine of the virgin birth of

Christ. The doctrine of the virgin birth and the doctrine of the deity of Christ are one and the same. The doctrine of the virgin birth and the doctrine of the blood atonement are so interrelated that they cannot be separated. They are Siamese-twin doctrines and neither doctrine can stand without the other. The virgin birth of Christ and His Saviourhood are one and the same doctrine.

Then anybody who denies the virgin birth of Christ is an infidel. He has already rejected Christianity. He has already denied the inspiration of the Bible. He has already denied the blood atonement of Christ. The man who denies the virgin birth of Christ may be counted a minister of the gospel, but actually he is a brother of Bob Ingersoll and Tom Paine, a brother of every infidel and Christ-denier and Bible-hater in the world.

If anyone says that the deity of Christ is not essential, then he does not even know what essential Christianity is. To deny the virgin birth is to deny Christ Himself!

I. The Virgin Birth Is Plainly Stated in Scripture

That the mother of Jesus was a virgin when He was conceived, not having known any man carnally, and a virgin still when the Saviour was born, is as specifically and positively stated as any doctrine in the Bible. Please consider the following Scripture statements about the virgin birth.

1. *Isaiah prophesied the Saviour's virgin birth some 740 years before it happened!* In Isaiah 7: 14 the Scripture says, "Therefore the Lord himself shall give you

a sign; Behold, a virgin shall conceive, and bear a son, and shall call his name Immanuel." The sign is given, as the preceding verse shows, to the whole house of David. A young woman was to conceive and bear a Son while she was yet a virgin, and should call His name Immanuel, meaning "God with us." This Child, virgin-born, was to be God incarnate, God dwelling for a little while with men!

2. *Matthew, the first Gospel, plainly teaches the virgin birth of Christ.* Read the following beautiful account of how God explained to Joseph how his sweetheart, Mary, was to become the mother of our Lord.

"Now the birth of Jesus Christ was on this wise: When as his mother Mary was espoused to Joseph, before they came together, she was found with child of the Holy Ghost. Then Joseph her husband, being a just man, and not willing to make her a publick example, was minded to put her away privily. But while he thought on these things, behold, the angel of the Lord appeared unto him in a dream, saying, Joseph, thou son of David, fear not to take unto thee Mary thy wife: for that which is conceived in her is of the Holy Ghost. And she shall bring forth a son, and thou shalt call his name JESUS: for he shall save his people from their sins. Now all this was done, that it might be fulfilled which was spoken of the Lord by the prophet, saying, Behold, a virgin shall be with child, and shall bring forth a son, and they shall call his name Emmanuel, which being interpreted is, God with us. Then Joseph being raised from sleep did as the angel of the Lord had bidden him, and took unto him his wife: And knew her not till she had brought

forth her firstborn son: and he called his name JESUS."
—Matt. 1: 18-25.

The Gospel of Matthew is recognized as the first Gospel written. The traditional date of the writing of Matthew's Gospel is A.D. 37, probably four years after the crucifixion. Even modernists all agree that the Gospel according to Matthew was the first one written. And this Gospel gives the longest and most detailed account of the virgin birth, and it quotes Isaiah 7: 14 and announces that that Scripture was fulfilled! The simple explanation is that the child in the womb of Mary was conceived by the Holy Ghost. God was literally the Father of our Lord Jesus Christ and so Jesus was "God with us," Immanuel. The same Scripture plainly announces that "thou shalt call his name JESUS: for he shall save his people from their sins."

A Christ who is virgin-born is the Saviour. A Christ not born of a virgin, a Christ with only a human father and a natural conception and birth, could never be a Saviour.

3. *The Gospel of Luke, written by "the beloved physician," Luke, also plainly states the fact of the virgin birth.* Read the following in Luke 1: 26-38.

"And in the sixth month the angel Gabriel was sent from God unto a city of Galilee, named Nazareth, To a virgin espoused to a man whose name was Joseph, of the house of David; and the virgin's name was Mary. And the angel came in unto her, and said, Hail, thou that art highly favoured, the Lord is with thee: blessed art thou among women. And when she saw him, she was troubled at his saying, and cast in her mind what manner of

*salutation this should be.   And the angel said unto her,
Fear not, Mary: for thou hast found favour with God.
And, behold, thou shalt conceive in thy womb, and bring
forth a son, and shalt call his name JESUS.   He shall
be great, and shall be called the Son of the Highest: and
the Lord God shall give unto him the throne of his father
David: And he shall reign over the house of Jacob for
ever; and of his kingdom there shall be no end.   Then
said Mary unto the angel, How shall this be, seeing I
know not a man?   And the angel answered and said unto
her, The Holy Ghost shall come upon thee, and the power
of the Highest shall overshadow thee: therefore also that
holy thing which shall be born of thee shall be called the
Son of God.   And, behold, thy cousin Elisabeth, she hath
also conceived a son in her old age: and this is the sixth
month with her, who was called barren.   For with God
nothing shall be impossible.   And Mary said, Behold the
handmaid of the Lord; be it unto me according to thy
word.   And the angel departed from her."*

Here again we are plainly told that Mary was a virgin
(vs. 27), that she was engaged to Joseph.   The problem
of how she should bear a child without a human father
troubled Mary, and the angel explained, "The Holy
Ghost shall come upon thee, and the power of the Highest shall overshadow thee: therefore also that holy thing
which shall be born of thee shall be called the Son of
God."   The virgin birth was essential were Christ to
be actually the Son of God, that is, physically begotten
of God and God in human form.

Obviously the doctrine of the virgin birth of Christ
is as clearly stated as any doctrine in the Bible.

II. The Virgin Birth Is Also Taught Elsewhere in the Bible Besides the Explicit Statements

Above we have seen that Isaiah, Matthew and Luke all expressly state that Christ was born of a virgin. But a number of other Scriptures, without using the term "virgin," clearly teach that Joseph was not the father of Jesus and that therefore He was conceived of the Holy Ghost, without a human father.

1. *The prophet Jeremiah plainly foretold that Joseph could not be the father of Jesus.* Here is a most interesting study that will repay careful attention. Jeremiah 22: 30 says of Coniah (also called Jeconiah, Jechonias and Jehoiachin), "Thus saith the Lord, Write ye this man childless, a man that shall not prosper in his days: for no man of his seed shall prosper, sitting upon the throne of David, and ruling any more in Judah."

And only five verses below this statement that Coniah, or Jeconiah, should be counted childless, that none of his seed should prosper reigning upon the throne of David, the Lord tells us, "Behold, the days come, saith the Lord, that I will raise unto David a righteous Branch, and a King shall reign and prosper, and shall execute judgment and justice in the earth" (Jer. 23: 5). And in the following verse we are told that His name should be called "THE LORD OUR RIGHTEOUSNESS."

Although Coniah's seed should not reign and prosper on David's throne, the coming Messiah would come and reign on David's throne. So the coming Saviour could not be descended from Jeconias.

But what does this have to do with the virgin birth of Christ? Simply this, that this man Coniah was the

ancestor of Joseph, the husband of Mary! Coniah, or
Jechonias, was a direct descendant of King Solomon and
King David, and reigned in Judah until he was carried
away captive to Babylon. Now look at the genealogy of
Joseph in Matthew 1: 12, "And after they were brought
to Babylon, Jechonias begat Salathiel. . . ." Then Matthew 1: 16, continuing the same genealogy, says, "And
Jacob begat Joseph the husband of Mary, of whom was
born Jesus, who is called Christ." Joseph was descended
from Coniah (Jechonias), and if Joseph were the father
of Jesus, then the Scripture plainly says that no one of
this line should prosper, sitting upon the throne of David
and ruling any more in Judah.

But in Luke 1: 32, 33 the angel Gabriel told Mary
about the Saviour, that great Son she should bear, "He
shall be great, and shall be called the Son of the Highest:
and the Lord God shall give unto him the throne of his
father David: And he shall reign over the house of
Jacob for ever; and of his kingdom there shall be no end."
Jesus, during His earthly ministry, of course, did not
reign in Judah nor over Jerusalem. But Jesus is coming
again, and the Lord God will give Him the throne of His
father David, and He will rule over the house of Jacob as
the Scripture clearly said. Revelation 5: 10 says, "And
hast made us unto our God kings and priests: and we shall
reign on the earth." Revelation 20: 6 says that those in
the first resurrection "shall be priests of God and of
Christ, and shall reign with him a thousand years."
Christ is to reign on David's throne.

Was it clearly intended by the Holy Spirit who dic-
tated the Scriptures that Jeremiah 22: 30 should be used

as proof that Jesus was not the son of Joseph? Yes, it was obviously so. For after Jeremiah 22: 30 says that no man of the seed of Coniah "shall prosper, sitting upon the throne of David, and ruling any more in Judah," the fifth and sixth verses thereafter, Jeremiah 23: 5, 6 say,

"Behold, the days come, saith the Lord, that I will raise unto David a righteous Branch, and a King shall reign and prosper, and shall execute judgment and justice in the earth. In his days Judah shall be saved, and Israel shall dwell safely: and this is his name whereby he shall be called, THE LORD OUR RIGHTEOUSNESS."

No seed of Coniah should reign and prosper in Judah; but Christ, "THE LORD OUR RIGHTEOUSNESS," *shall* reign and prosper on David's throne ruling over Judah and the whole earth! So Coniah, the ancestor of Joseph, could not be the ancestor of Jesus. Jesus was not born of Joseph!

2. *The genealogy of Jesus, through Mary, does not give Coniah (Jechonias) at all, proving that Jesus was descended from David through another line, not Joseph's line.* We have mentioned the genealogy of "Joseph the husband of Mary," which is given in Matthew 1: 1-16. But the genealogy of Mary is given in Luke 3: 23-38. At first glance one might think that this was the genealogy of Joseph and wonder why the two were different. Matthew 1: 16 says, "And Jacob begat Joseph the husband of Mary." But in Luke 3: 23 we are told, "And Jesus himself began to be about thirty years of age, being (as was supposed) the son of Joseph, which was *the son* of Heli." Actually, the words "the son," used the

second time in this verse, are in italics, meaning they were not in the Greek at all. Actually there is no doubt that Joseph was *son-in-law* of Heli. The Gospel of Matthew speaks of Jesus as the King of the Jews, and so gives the genealogy of Joseph, His foster father, as an official record showing that, humanly speaking, He would be entitled to the throne of Israel. The Gospel of Matthew was more clearly directed to the Jews. But the gospel according to Luke pictures Jesus as the Son of man, and gives His genealogy, not just to Abraham the father of Jews, as does the genealogy in Matthew, but traces it all the way back to Adam! So the genealogy in Luke naturally gives the actual human parentage of Jesus, that is, His mother Mary and her ancestry.

The Scofield Reference Bible has a note on Luke 3:23 as follows: "In Matthew, where unquestionably we have the genealogy of Joseph, we are told (1:16) that Joseph was the son of Jacob. In what sense, then, could he be called in Luke 'the son of Heli'? He could not be by natural generation the son both of Jacob and of Heli. But in Luke it is not said that Heli *begat* Joseph, so that the natural explanation is that Joseph was the son-in-law of Heli, who was, like himself, a descendant of David. That he should in that case be called 'son of Heli' ('son' is not in the Greek, but rightly supplied by the translators) would be in accord with Jewish usage (cf. I Sam. 24:16). The conclusion is therefore inevitable that in Luke we have Mary's genealogy; and Joseph was '*son* of Heli' because espoused to Heli's daughter. The genealogy in Luke is Mary's, whose father, Heli, was decended from David."

Now note this interesting thing. The genealogy of Mary, and therefore the literal human genealogy of Christ, is not traced through Coniah (Jechonias) at all. It is not even traced through King Solomon, but is traced through Nathan, another son of David! (Luke 3: 31). Jesus was actually, literally descended, through Mary, from King David. But He was not descended from Jechonias. God gave that additional proof in the Old Testament, before the Saviour was born, that Joseph could not be His father.

3. *The Scripture repeatedly speaks of Jesus as the only One who was begotten of God, "the only begotten Son of God."* This clearly refers to the fact that Jesus was born of a virgin, with God as His Father. The Scripture tells us that "Jacob begat Joseph the husband of Mary" (Matt. 1: 16), but many Scriptures tell us that God begot Jesus Christ. Psalm 2: 7 prophesies the coming of the Saviour and says, "The Lord hath said unto me, Thou art my Son; this day have I begotten thee." All Bible students agree that that refers to Jesus Christ. Now Jesus was in the very beginning with God. John 1: 1-3 says, "In the beginning was the Word, and the Word was with God, and the Word was God. The same was in the beginning with God. All things were made by him; and without him was not any thing made that was made." If Jesus was in the beginning with the Father, then surely it could not be said that He ever had a beginning, in His pre-existent state with the Father. So when we speak of Jesus as "the only begotten Son" of God, we refer to His human beginning. On the mother's side we say

that a child is conceived. On the father's side we say that the child is begotten. So when the Holy Spirit overshadowed Mary, God begot Jesus Christ, and therefore He is called the only begotten Son of God. No one else was ever physically begotten by God, as Jesus was, so He is "the only begotten Son."

The first chapter of John has much to say about Jesus as the pre-existent Word of God, as the Creator of all things. John 1: 14 says, "And the Word was made flesh, and dwelt among us, (and we beheld his glory, the glory as of the only begotten of the Father,) full of grace and truth." When the Word was made flesh, that is, when Christ was made flesh, then He was begotten of the Father; and what the beloved John is here saying by divine inspiration is that they, the disciples, beheld the glory of Christ, and could tell by His glory that He was deity, that He was physically begotten of God! John means that anyone who saw the glorified Saviour on the Mount of Transfiguration, and again after His resurrection, as well as all the days of His ministry, would have to agree that Jesus had no human father, but was begotten of God and conceived and borne by a virgin mother.

It is true that once or twice the Bible speaks of Christians as begotten of God, but that is a figurative use of the term, and five times in the New Testament Jesus is called the *only* begotten Son of God. Those five times are John 1: 14; John 1: 18; John 3: 16; John 3: 18; and I John 4: 9. So the Gospel of John and the first epistle of John unite with the books of Isaiah and Matthew and Luke in declaring the virgin birth of our Saviour!

4. *Another reference to the virgin birth of Christ is given in Jeremiah 31:22.* There in a prophecy of the coming Saviour the prophet says, "How long wilt thou go about, O thou backsliding daughter? for the Lord hath created a new thing in the earth, A woman shall compass a man."

Certainly it would not be a new thing for a woman to conceive and bear a man child. That is not what God means. No, he says, "The Lord hath created a new thing in the earth," an entirely new thing would happen. That is, a woman, without any human intervention, without knowing any man carnally, would "compass a man," that is, conceive and carry and deliver a man child! That virgin birth of Christ would be a unique event, a wholly new thing. Certainly this must be a reference to the virgin birth of the coming Saviour.

III. The Virgin Birth Is Implied All Through the Bible

I have shown that the virgin birth is expressly stated in Isaiah, Matthew and Luke, and that it is taught elsewhere very clearly. But that is not all. The birth of Jesus without a human father and His deity as a result is implied all through the Bible. I have mentioned three of the Gospels: Matthew and Luke expressly say that Jesus was born of a virgin, and John expressly says that Jesus was begotten of God and was the only person ever begotten of God, was God's only begotten Son. However, the Gospel of Mark leaves no room for doubt on this question. While it does not expressly state that

Jesus was born of a virgin, it emphatically teaches that
Jesus was the pre-existent Son of God which necessarily
means that He was not the son of Joseph.

Mark 1 : 1 says, "The beginning of the gospel of Jesus
Christ, the Son of God." The first word that Mark has
to say about the Saviour is that He is the Son of God!
And the first chapter only proceeds to the eleventh verse
before it reports God saying from heaven, "Thou art
my beloved Son, in whom I am well pleased." And all
through the Gospel of Mark Jesus is spoken of as the
miracle-working God in human form. That necessarily
means that He was born of a virgin. Although Mark
does not tell the story of the angel's coming to Mary
and of the Saviour's miraculous conception and birth,
that truth is implied throughout the Gospel.

So it is all through the Bible. In Isaiah 9: 6 it is
prophesied, "For unto us a child is born, unto us a son
is given: and the government shall be upon his shoulder:
and his name shall be called Wonderful, Counsellor, The
mighty God, The everlasting Father, The Prince of
Peace." Though this verse does not specially tell of
the virgin birth of Christ, it calls him "The mighty God,
The everlasting Father." And that forever sets Him
apart from every man child ever born of natural generation, and necessarily compels a belief in the deity of
Christ.

Isaiah 53 tells of the atonement; how Christ bore our
griefs and carried our sorrows, how He was wounded
for our transgressions and bruised for our iniquities,
and how the chastisement of our peace was upon Him
and how with His stripes we are healed. If one Man

can stand before God for the whole race of men, and if one Man's suffering can pay the debt of all the sinners in the universe, then that one Man is no ordinary man. He could only be a God-man, God in human form, begotten of God in a virgin's womb. That is why all those who deny the virgin birth of Christ likewise deny His deity and deny His atoning death, His substitutionary sacrifice for our sins.

Throughout the Bible we are taught that Christ is the Creator who made all things and upholds all things now. We are taught that He is to judge the world, and that the Father has committed all judgment to the Son (John 5: 22; Acts 17: 31). We are told that the same Jesus who was crucified arose from the dead. We are told that He ascended to Heaven and then two angels promised that the same Jesus should return again (Acts 1: 9-11). Jesus Himself said, "If I go and prepare a place for you, I will come again, and receive you unto myself" (John 14: 3). "In him dwelleth all the fulness of the Godhead bodily" (Col. 2: 9).

The virgin birth is implied in every chapter in the Bible, and to deny the virgin birth of Christ is to deny that the Bible means what it says, to deny that it is the Word of God. To deny the virgin birth is to deny historic Christianity and turn one's back on the God of the Bible.

IV. Objections to the Virgin Birth Answered

Unbelievers, haters of the Bible and rejectors of Christ object to the Bible doctrine of the virgin birth. But their objections are not sensible as investigation will prove.

1. *They say, "It is only mentioned in two or three places in the Bible."* That is not true. We have shown that the virgin birth is plainly taught in Isaiah, Jeremiah, Matthew, Luke, John, and the first epistle of John, and is implied throughout the Scriptures everywhere. If it were only stated one time in the Bible, that would be enough for any Christian. But the virgin birth is as clearly taught as any Bible doctrine, and is often repeated.

2. *"Jesus Himself did not claim to be born of a virgin," says the modernist and infidel.* That is simply not true. Those who deny the virgin birth are not scholarly and they do not know what the Bible really teaches. Jesus clearly said, "For the bread of God is he which cometh down from heaven, and giveth life unto the world" (John 6: 33) ; and then He said, "I am that bread of life" (John 6: 48). Jesus said that He came down from Heaven. That could not be said of any other man in the world. That involved His pre-existence with God the Father and His deity, and necessarily presumes that God begot Him at His conception. Jesus plainly called Himself the "only begotten Son" of God (John 3:16). He was the only Man ever begotten physically by God. Jesus told Nicodemus that He, Jesus, was "He that came down from heaven, even the Son of man which is in heaven" (John 3: 13). To the Pharisees, Jesus plainly said, "Ye are from beneath; I am from above: ye are of this world; I am not of this world. I said therefore unto you, that ye shall die in your sins: for if ye believe not that I am he, ye shall die in your sins" (John 8: 23, 24). Jesus said

that He came from above, that He was not of this world as other men were, and that therefore He was God and that anyone who would not believe Him to be what He claimed to be, God in human form, should die in his sins! The virgin birth, the deity of Christ, and salvation by faith in Him, are all taught in these words of Jesus Christ. Certainly He claimed to be the virgin-born Son of God!

And all the enemies of Christ in His own lifetime knew that was what He claimed. John 5:18 says, "Therefore the Jews sought the more to kill him, because he not only had broken the sabbath, but said also that God was his Father, making himself equal with God" (John 5:18). Jesus certainly claimed deity, insisted that He was begotten of God, that is, virgin-born, and came down from Heaven, as no other man did.

3. *"But scientists cannot believe in the virgin birth of Christ because there are no scientific records of any other case of one being born without a human father,"* says some scoffer. Indeed! But we are not claiming that men are born every few days without a human father! We are not claiming that anybody else was ever born of a virgin. In fact, we are claiming just the opposite, that Jesus is the only person ever so conceived and born with a virgin mother and without a human father. We are not talking about an ordinary man, but a God-man, God incarnate in human flesh! If you should tell me that any scientist or statesman, any genius or philanthropist of this day were born of a virgin, I would not believe you. If you should tell me that any of them rose from the dead, I would laugh at you. The late

President Roosevelt, for example, was a man. He attained high honor, but nevertheless he was only a man, born as were other men, and dying like other men. There was nothing about Roosevelt to indicate that he was God, that he created the world, that he will one day be judge of all the universe. The virgin birth would not fit Franklin D. Roosevelt nor any other man who ever lived. It does fit Jesus Christ who is God in human form.

A few years ago scientists announced that by the use of an electric impulse, the ova of a female rabbit had been stimulated into growth and development and that this mother rabbit had borne a baby rabbit without intercourse with a male rabbit. In other words, scientists were able to induce the virgin birth of a rabbit. They have not been able to produce the same effect on a human ova. But what scientists did by an electrical impulse in the womb of a rabbit, could not the Almighty God do in the conception of His Son Jesus Christ in the womb of a virgin? The virgin birth fits the nature and the life of Jesus Christ, and it is easy for anybody to believe who accepts Jesus as what He claimed to be, the Son of God who came into the world to save sinners.

4. *"But that would be a miracle, and I cannot believe in miracles," says an unbeliever.* A miracle? Certainly! But sensible scientists have long ago decided that only miracles could account for many things. Where did matter come from? It was created by a miracle, of course. How were the planetary systems arranged and balanced and set it motion? Unquestionably by some miracle of God. And how did life originate and begin? No scientist in the world now believes that life can come from

dead matter of itself. Scientists believe that the earth
was once a fiery mass where life could not exist. They
know that now life is on this planet. Where did it come
from? Without any other explanation possible, life came
as a miracle of God's creation. One who cannot believe
in miracles is an ignoramus and an unthinking enemy
of fact.

A miracle, the conception of Christ and His virgin
birth? Certainly! Christ Himself is the God of miracles. He worked many, many miracles Himself. He
died for our sins, died as no one else ever died, and then
miraculously rose from the dead. Miraculously He appeared to the disciples and then ascended visibly to Heav-
en. He is coming again. The Bible is a miracle. Creation was a miracle. Every time a soul is regenerated
and made into a new creature, that is a miracle. Certainly the virgin birth of Christ is a miracle.

I heard Dr. L. R. Scarborough, the late president of
the Southwestern Baptist Theological Seminary at Fort
Worth, tell in our class in evangelism in the seminary
how one of his sons, only six or eight years old at the
time, came home from Sunday School one day. "Dad,
I don't believe that stuff they told us today about a whale
swallowing Jonah," said the small boy.

"But, son, if God could make a whale and could make
a man, why couldn't God make the whale swallow the
man and keep the man alive three days in the whale?"
asked Dr. Scarborough.

"Oh, well," said the boy, "if you are going to put
God in it, I can believe it, too!"

So like that lad, if you put God in it, I can believe in

the virgin birth. And everybody who puts God in it has to believe in the virgin birth. If Jesus was God come in human form, the only begotten Son of God, then of course that means He was born of a virgin, as the Bible says. Certainly that is a miracle, but the Bible is a miracle book, and Christianity is a miracle religion, and no one can be a Christian who does not believe in these essential miracles.

5. *"But intelligent people do not believe in the virgin birth," some ungodly teacher tells the innocent young people in his class.* He could not face an intelligent and informed Christian leader on such a question, but he sets out to break down the faith of boys and girls with immature minds, parroting infidelity because he is against God and the Bible and has not made any honest investigation. But what is true? Do intelligent and educated people believe in the virgin birth?

The answer is that every great creed in Christendom has stood for the virgin birth of Christ, from the Apostle's Creed on down to the Westminster Confession or the New Hampshire statement of faith. All the apostles believed, of course, in the virgin birth. All the great church fathers, all the reformers, including Martin Luther, John Calvin, and John Wesley, believed in the virgin birth. All the great teachers and preachers of Christianity — Spurgeon, Moody, Finney, Torrey — all the great Bible-believing theologians and evangelists and pastors and students have agreed on the virgin birth of Christ. The only people who deny the virgin birth are infidels who do not believe the Bible, do not believe in the deity of Christ, and do not trust Him as their own personal Saviour. Modernists, infidels, those who join Bob Ingersoll, Voltaire, Tom Paine, and Hitler, of course, deny the virgin birth. But no true Christian in the world denies the virgin birth. Great scientists like Sir Isaac Newton, Sir James Simpson, Lord Kelvin, Louis Pasteur, and statesmen like Gladstone, Lloyd George, Winston Churchill, George Washington, Abraham Lincoln, Woodrow Wilson, Herbert Hoover and William Jennings Bryan have believed in the deity of Jesus Christ and in His virgin birth. Everywhere that good men, profoundly intelligent men, love the Lord Jesus and believe the Word of God, they believe in the virgin birth of Christ as taught so plainly in the Scriptures.

Then let every Christian be happy in his faith. You have the best wisdom, the best character, the greatest fellowship of the ages on your side. And if all the world besides still denied the virgin birth of Christ, any Christian who has been born again, who knows Christ as a personal Saviour, would know that He is all He claimed to be, the virgin-born Son of God.

Let us teach the virgin birth to our children. It is a beautiful mystery, a holy mystery that they can believe and grasp. Let all of God's people give to the dear Lord Jesus the reverence and worship which belong to Him as the Creator of the world, God come in human form, born of a virgin, living a perfect, sinless life, dying for our sins on the cross, buried and rising again from the dead and ascending into the heavens, and one day to return again to receive us to Himself!

Chapter 4

OLD TESTAMENT PROPHECIES MIRACULOUSLY FULFILLED IN CHRIST

"Then he said unto them, O fools, and slow of heart to believe all that the prophets have spoken: Ought not Christ to have suffered these things, and to enter into his glory? And beginning at Moses and all the prophets, he expounded unto them in all the scriptures the things concerning himself."—Luke 24: 25-27.

It was Jesus Himself, walking toward Emmaus with two disciples who did not recognize Him and who did not believe that He had risen from the dead, who rebuked them for their unbelief. Jesus said to them, "O fools, and slow of heart to believe all that the prophets have spoken." Then Jesus went through the Old Testament Scriptures which He knew so well and told them of prophecy after prophecy that concerned His coming, His life, His death, His resurrection. And Jesus said that anybody who was even slow to believe the Scriptures was a fool! He Himself was the fulfillment of so many prophecies that only one spiritually wicked, spiritually a fool, would be slow to believe that He was the Christ of God, Emmanuel, "God with us," God's only begotten Son. Only spiritual fools can doubt that these fulfillments of prophecy prove the Bible to be the Word of God.

Many, many intricate details of the birth, life, ministry, death, and resurrection of Jesus are foretold in the Old Testament so definitely that their fulfillment could not be accidental.

Suppose that you had a book written by a series of prophets and saints through several centuries but all of them agreeing perfectly; suppose this book were accepted by the most devout and honorable, the saintliest people of the world, as God's own book; suppose that all the writers claimed that they verily spake the words of God. Now suppose that in this book centuries old it was told again and again that God would send a saviour, a deliverer, His own son into the world. Suppose that the year of his coming were exactly given as 483 years from a certain event. Suppose the village of his birth were named, the family line into which he would be born. Suppose the very day of the month and the time of day of his death were described in detail. Suppose that dozens of events in his life were foretold, even to his own words and his death, and the very words of his enemies. Then suppose you saw these things take place. Suppose every detail prophesied were fulfilled to the letter. Would you not know that surely the book we have mentioned was God's Book, and the person described was God's Son, the Saviour? That is actually the kind of evidence we have about the deity of Jesus Christ. Actually the proof is much more detailed and exact and conclusive than I have indicated. The prophecies concerning Jesus Christ and their fulfillment prove that Jesus Christ is indeed God's own Son and is deity Himself incarnate. And the same evidence proves that the Bible is as it claims to be, the very Word of God, supernaturally inspired and trustworthy.   And Jesus Christ Himself said that only a fool with a spiritually slow heart could be slow to believe all that the prophets have spoken about Him!

The last book of the Old Testament, Malachi, is dated nearly four hundred years before the birth of Christ. Every book in the Old Testament had been written so long that the Jews had a definitely established canon of the Old Testament, and the entire Old Testament had been translated into Greek by a group of seventy Jewish scholars, 278 to 270 B.C., long years before Christ came. Of all the critics of the Bible, all the infidel scholars, not one denies that the entire Old Testament was completed long before Jesus Christ was born.   Hence, if the Old Testament foretells accurately the literal events connected with the birth and life and death of Christ, there is only one possible explanation.   That explanation is that the Old Testament is the inspired Word of God and that God Himself revealed ahead of time the events that would happen.   That is exactly what we find to be the case.

Throughout the Old Testament there are definite prophecies about a coming Person.   Jewish scholars had discovered, long before the Saviour came, that many, many separate promises all pointed to the coming of the same Person.   They called that coming Person the Messiah.   He was the 'Seed of the woman that should bruise the serpent's head and the serpent should bruise his heel,' as promised to Adam and Eve in Genesis 3: 15. He was the promised 'Seed of Abraham in whom all the

kindred of the earth should be blessed' (Gen. 12: 1-3).
He was the 'Prophet like unto Moses' who was promised
in Deuteronomy 18: 15.   He was the One pictured in
all the sacrifices as dying for the sins of others.   He was
the 'Anointed' of Psalm 2: 2, the 'Son' of Psalm 2: 12,
the 'Servant' of Isaiah 52: 13, and of all the fifty-third
chapter of Isaiah.   He was the 'Messiah the Prince' of
Daniel 9: 25.   Orthodox Jews today know that the Old
Testament foretells in many, many places the coming of
a Messiah, a Prince or Saviour.   They may harden their
hearts and go on in sin and reject the Saviour just as
other lost sinners do; but every honest inquirer, either
Jew or Gentile, who searches for the Messiah foretold in
the Old Testament, may find Him revealed in the New
Testament, and every prophecy concerning His first coming already meticulously fulfilled!

And for readers who are not scholars let us say that
the important historical outlines of the birth, life and
death of Christ are now proved.   There is as much proof
that a man named Jesus was born and lived and was
crucified in Palestine early in the first century, as there
is evidence for the birth, life and death of George Washington in the eighteenth century.   Unconverted Jewish
scholars, who do not accept Christ as their Saviour, do
acknowledge that such a Person lived and did wonderful
things in Palestine.   Mohammedans are not Christian
and do not accept Christ as the Saviour.   They have their
own bible, the Koran, and do not accept the New Testament.   Yet they know Jesus Christ as a historical per-
sonage and accept Him as a prophet.   Josephus, a great
Jewish writer, widely accepted as a secular historian,

gives many details concerning the life of Christ, John the Baptist, and other people who lived in Palestine during the life of Christ. So Jesus Christ is a proved historical character.

That means that when the Gospels—Matthew, Mark, Luke and John—in the New Testament were written, they could be checked by hundreds of thousands of people who would know the facts concerning many important details in the life of Christ. The Lord Jesus preached to many thousands of people. His trial and execution were public, state affairs. Events like the coming of the wise men, Herod's slaughter of innocent children, the rending of the temple vail, the three hours of darkness and the earthquake when Jesus died were all matters known to multiplied thousands. And these essentials of the life of Christ are not contradicted by any historian or writer, whether Jew or Roman, infidel or Mohammedan.

So—knowing that the historical events mentioned in the New Testament have been checked and proved reliable on the whole, uncontradicted by any scholars; and knowing that the Old Testament was written long before—we need only to compare the facts with the Old Testament prophecies to see whether Jesus is really the Messiah, and whether the Bible is truly the infallible Word of God. And the proof which I give is overwhelming. Those who search for the truth can find it. I challenge men of honest minds to see for themselves whether the historic Christ of the New Testament was miraculously foretold in the Old Testament. If so, the Bible is the Word of God.

A. Details of the Birth of Christ Foretold

1. The Saviour Must Descend From Abraham, From Judah, From King David

Genesis 12: 2, 3 tells how God said to Abraham: "And I will make of thee a great nation, and I will bless thee, and make thy name great; and thou shalt be a blessing: And I will bless them that bless thee, and curse him that curseth thee: and in thee shall all families of the earth be blessed." That promise could not possibly be true of any other man but of Christ, Abraham's seed according to the flesh. So Jews properly counted this as teaching that the coming Messiah should be descended from Abraham. Galatians 3: 8 says: "And the scripture, foreseeing that God would justify the heathen through faith, preached before the gospel unto Abraham, saying, In thee shall all nations be blessed."

In Genesis 13: 15 God promised to Abraham, concerning the land of Canaan, "For all the land which thou seest, to thee will I give it, and to thy seed for ever." A similar promise is given in Genesis 15: 18, and in Genesis 17: 8. The word *seed* in Genesis 13: 15 is not in the plural but singular form, referring to one descendant of Abraham who would possess the land of Canaan forever. In the same context the plural form is used referring to the Jewish nation, but Galatians 3: 16 in the New Testament calls attention to the singular form and says, "Now to Abraham and his seed were the promises made. He saith not, And to seeds, as of many; but as of one, And to thy seed, which is Christ." So the coming Saviour had to be of Abraham's seed, and He would come to possess the land of Canaan and rule it. Many Scriptures make clear that that reign is in the future. It is sufficient for our purposes here to show that the coming Messiah must be descended from Abraham.

But Christ also must be descended from Judah. In Genesis 49: 10 the prophecy which God gave Jacob about his sons is quoted as follows: "The sceptre shall not depart from Judah, nor a lawgiver from between his feet, until Shiloh come; and unto him shall the gathering of the people be." The word *Shiloh* means rest, or Messiah. This Messiah or Lawgiver to whom the people would be gathered must be descended from Judah.

The promise was even more explicit. The coming Messiah must come from the kingly line of David. In II Samuel 7: 16 God said to David, through the prophet Nathan, "And thine house and thy kingdom shall be established for ever before thee: thy throne shall be established for ever." That clear promise is repeated in the eighty-ninth Psalm, verse 4, and in I Chronicles 22: 10. Now the reign of Christ was not prophesied to occur at His first coming. Jesus came the first time to die, and the Bible tells that He will come the second time to reign. But the important point here is that God prophesied that this coming Messiah, the seed of Abraham, the Shiloh and Lawgiver from Judah, would be of the house of David.

Now here is the remarkable fulfillment. The first sentence in the New Testament is this: "The book of the generation of Jesus Christ, the son of David, the son of Abraham." And there follows a detailed genealogy showing that Jesus came through Abraham, Isaac and

Judah, *officially*—that is, by adoption—since that is the genealogy of Joseph, the foster father of Jesus, but not His real father. And then the literal and real genealogy of the Lord Jesus is given in Luke 3: 23-38, from Eli, Mary's father, the father-in-law of Joseph and the human grandfather of the Lord Jesus, all the way back through King David, Judah, and Abraham!

2. Christ Was to Be Born at Bethlehem in Judea

Micah 5: 2 says, "But thou, Bethlehem Ephratah, though thou be little among the thousands of Judah, yet out of thee shall he come forth unto me that is to be ruler in Israel; whose goings forth have been from of old, from everlasting." The Jews all understood this to refer to the Saviour. So, in the New Testament, when the wise men came from the East to inquire about the Christ who had been born, Herod had the chief priests and scribes gathered, and they instructed the wise men to seek for the baby Jesus in Bethlehem, because of this verse (Matt. 2: 3-8). And in Bethlehem they found the baby Jesus. See also Luke 2: 1-7.

This is a startling fact, that the very village where the Saviour was to be born was foretold. A very dear friend of mine, Louis Zuckerman, had spent eight years in a school of the Talmud, preparing to be a Jewish rabbi, before leaving Russia for the United States. In Chicago he taught in the Hebrew Institute as a Hebrew scholar. But familiar as he was with the Old Testament in the original Hebrew, he had never noticed Micah 5: 2, promising that the Messiah should be born in Bethlehem in Judea, until he heard it in the First Methodist Church in Dallas, Texas. He stormed out of the church declaring that the preacher was a liar, deceiving the people, that no such promise was in the Old Testament. But back in his room he looked in his Hebrew Old Testament and there it was! As a result of that verse, he was convinced that Christ was the Messiah, accepted Him as his Saviour and soon thereafter became my intimate friend and was often in my home. No one denies that Jesus was born in Bethlehem. No one can deny that it was foretold hundreds of years before, in Micah 5:2.

3. The Very Year of Christ's Coming Was Foretold

Here is a little-known but startling truth. The ninth chapter of Daniel has a definite prophecy that Christ would come 483 years after a certain decree by a Medo-Persian king! When that world ruler should order Jerusalem restored and rebuilt, in the days of Nehemiah, 483 years would then ensue until Messiah, the Prince, should appear! Daniel 9:25 says:

"Know therefore and understand, that from the going forth of the commandment to restore and to build Jerusalem unto the Messiah the Prince shall be seven weeks, and threescore and two weeks: the street shall be built again, and the wall, even in troublous times."

Remember that Jews had weeks of years the same as weeks of days. After sixty-nine sevens of years (7 plus 62 by 7). or 483 years, the Messiah the Prince was to be manifested.

That amazing prophecy was written hundreds of years before Christ came, and it was literally fulfilled. Some parts of the context have to do with Christ's *second* coming. But the 483 years between the king's command to build and restore Jerusalem and the coming of the Saviour, have been fulfilled, and I have never even heard of an infidel who claimed he could disprove this fact. It was no doubt because the wise men in Babylon had read this very passage from Daniel the prophet that they were looking for the Messiah when He was born in Bethlehem of Judea, as discussed in the second chapter of Matthew.

4. Herod's Slaughter of Innocent Babies and the Flight With the Baby Jesus Into Egypt Were Foretold

In Hosea 11: 1 we read, "When Israel was a child, then I loved him, and called my son out of Egypt." On the surface, that verse is about Israel, the nation. But a nation is not a son. In the second Psalm the coming Christ, the Anointed, is discussed, and verse twelve says, "Kiss the Son, lest he be angry, and ye perish from the way, when his wrath is kindled but a little. Blessed are all they that put their trust in him." Clearly the Messiah, the Son of God, is the one meant. And Hosea 11: 1 refers to this same Son of God! God would call His Son out of Egypt, Hosea prophesied!

That is exactly what happened. The wise men warned Joseph of Herod's plans to destroy the baby Jesus. Matthew 2: 14, 15 then tells us, "When he arose, he took the young child and his mother by night, and departed into Egypt: And was there until the death of Herod: that it might be fulfilled which was spoken of the Lord by the prophet, saying, Out of Egypt have I called my son." God's prophecy was fulfilled!

Herod, in anger, when the wise men would not help him find the baby Jesus, killed many innocent children. Matthew 2: 16-18 tells us,

"Then Herod, when he saw that he was mocked of the wise men, was exceeding wroth, and sent forth, and slew all the children that were in Bethlehem, and in all the coasts thereof, from two years old and under, according to the time which he had diligently enquired of the wise men. Then was fulfilled that which was spoken by Jeremy the prophet, saying, In Rama was there a voice heard, lamentation, and weeping, and great mourning, Rachel weeping for her children, and would not be comforted, because they are not."

The quotation from Jeremiah is in Jeremiah 31: 15. Hundreds of years before Jesus was born, the incident of the baby Jesus being carried down into Egypt and of Herod's terrible slaughter of the innocents was foretold by Hosea and Jeremiah.

Another marvelous fulfillment of prophecy was that Jesus was born of a virgin. Isaiah 7: 14 tells us, "Therefore the Lord himself shall give you a sign; Behold, a virgin shall conceive, and bear a son, and shall call his name Immanuel." How that prophecy was marvelously fulfilled, so that Jesus was born of a virgin without a human father, is told in detail in Matthew, chapter 1, and Luke, chapter 1. However, I do not here stress the point of Christ's virgin birth, since it is denied by those who deny the Bible. We are only stressing here those prophecies whose fulfillment is absolutely undeniable, which any infidel may check up on and find the prophecy and its literal fulfillment.

B. Many Literal Details of the Death of Christ Foretold in the Old Testament

1. It Was Foretold That Christ Must Die for Others, a Substitutionary, Atoning Death

Isaiah 53: 5, 6 states that clearly;

"But he was wounded for our transgressions, he was bruised for our iniquities: the chastisement of our peace was upon him; and with his stripes we are healed. All we like sheep have gone astray; we have turned every one to his own way; and the Lord hath laid on him the iniquity of us all."

That was the clear, prophetic meaning of the Passover lamb in Exodus, chapter 12. The scapegoat pictured Christ carrying away our sins. The bullock as a sacrifice pictured Christ, our burden-bearing Saviour. The mourning turtledove pictured Christ, the Man of sorrows and acquainted with grief. The white pigeon pictured Christ, the pure and innocent One, the stainless One, dying for others. And always the blood of animal sacrifices pictured the blood of Christ which would atone for man's sins. Leviticus 17: 11 says, "For the life of the flesh is in the blood: and I have given it to you upon the altar to make an atonement for your souls: for it is the blood that maketh an atonement for the soul."

The New Testament clearly tells that all these prophecies were fulfilled in Christ. Paul tells us in I Corinthians 15: 3, 4 that the gospel is this: "For I delivered unto you first of all that which I also received, how that Christ died for our sins according to the scriptures; And that he was buried, and that he arose again the third day according to the scriptures." First Corinthians 5: 7 says, "For even Christ our passover is sacrificed for us." Second Corinthians 5: 21 says, "For he hath made him to be sin for us, who knew no sin; that we might be made the righteousness of God in him." And this precious doctrine, that Christ fulfilled Old Testament prophecies in His atoning death on the cross, is plainly taught in I Peter 1: 18, 19, which says, "Forasmuch as ye know that ye were not redeemed with corruptible things, as silver and gold, from your vain conversation received by tradition from your fathers; But with the precious blood of Christ, as of a lamb without blemish and without spot."

2. The Messiah, the Saviour, Must Be Crucified, Hanged on a Wooden Cross

Since Christ was to bear the curse of all sinners, it was an easily-understood prophecy that He must be hanged, suspended publicly on the cross. Deuteronomy 21: 22, 23, says:

"And if a man have committed a sin worthy of death, and he be to be put to death, and thou hang him on a tree: His body shall not remain all night upon the tree, but thou shalt in any wise bury him that day; (for he that is hanged is accursed of God;) that thy land be not defiled, which the Lord thy God giveth thee for an inheritance."

Note that statement, "for he that is hanged is accursed of God." If Christ bore the curse of God for us, then it would have to be by some public hanging. So Jesus was crucified on a Roman cross. And Galatians

3: 13 explains it thus: "Christ hath redeemed us from the curse of the law, being made a curse for us: for it is written, Cursed is every one that hangeth on a tree."

But Christ must be *nailed* to the cross, as well as be hanged there. To hang Him with rope would not be enough to fulfill the Scriptures. Zechariah 13: 6 prophesies that in the future some who see Christ will say to Him, "What are these wounds in thine hands?" And we are told He will answer, "Those with which I was wounded in the house of my friends." Psalm 22: 16 says: "They pierced my hands and my feet." The nail-scars in the hands of Christ were prophesied in the Old Testament!

It is striking that Christ should be crucified instead of stoned, for when the Old Testament prophecies were written, crucifixion was unknown among the Jews. Even when people were hanged on the tree in Old Testament times, it was *after* they had been put to death, as you see from Deuteronomy 21: 22. The customary, almost universal manner of inflicting the official death penalty was by stoning. But the Old Testament Scriptures foretold that Christ would die by being nailed to a cross, and it came to pass, as each of the Gospels tells us. This unlikely event came to pass because God had inspired the prophecy and fulfilled it!

3. The Saviour Was Not to Have a Single Bone Broken

I have said that the Passover lamb pictured Christ, the coming Messiah. Every detail of that Passover lamb had a meaning. The lamb must be without spot or blemish (Exod. 12: 5), picturing the sinlessness of Christ.

It was roasted whole with fire, and eaten with bitter herbs, signifying the sufferings of Christ. And here is a startling fact. God insisted that when each family in Egypt would kill, roast and eat a Passover lamb each year, that they should never break a bone of it. Exodus 12: 46 says, "Neither shall ye break a bone thereof." So when the coming Saviour should appear and be rejected by Israel, it was prophesied that they should never break His bones.

How often the Jews intended to do that very thing! Again and again we are told that 'They took up stones to stone him' (John 8: 59; John 10: 31, etc.). But they never could do it! And when Jesus hung on the cross, Satan would have wished to break this prophecy and prove the Bible a lie. The Jews came and "besought Pilate that their legs [the legs of Jesus and the two thieves crucified with Him] might be broken, and that they might be taken away" (John 19: 31). But did the soldiers break the legs of Jesus, as the Jews demanded and as Pilate agreed? No! For verses 32 and 33 tell us, "Then came the soldiers, and brake the legs of the first, and of the other which was crucified with him. But when they came to Jesus, and saw that he was dead already, they brake not his legs." Then again, verse 36 in the same chapter says, "For these things were done, that the scripture should be fulfilled, A bone of him shall not be broken." How marvelous it is that these details of Old Testament prophecies were fulfilled to the very letter in Christ's death! The only satisfactory explanation of the detailed accuracy and literal fulfillment of the Old Testament prophecies is divine inspiration.

4. Yet the Dying Saviour Had to Be Pierced With a Spear

Since the death of Christ was to be of such matchless importance, many, many details concerning the death of the coming Messiah were foretold by Old Testament prophets. For example, Zechariah 12: 10 tells how the inhabitants of Jerusalem would one day look upon the Messiah whom they had pierced: "And I will pour upon the house of David, and upon the inhabitants of Jerusalem, the spirit of grace and of supplications: *and they shall look upon me whom they have pierced."* Now how was this fulfilled? Turn again to John 19 and we find that when the soldiers saw that Jesus was already dead and did not break His legs, then, verse 34 tells us, "one of the soldiers with a spear pierced his side, and forthwith came there out blood and water." Then verse 37 below explains the meaning of it thus, "And again another scripture saith, They shall look on him whom they pierced."

5. The Death-Scene of the Dying Saviour Is Pictured in Detail in Psalm 22

When the twenty-second Psalm was written, the Bible was certainly put to the test. If the details there so clearly pictured should be fulfilled in the death of the coming Messiah, the Bible would be forever proved as the infallible Word of God. And that is exactly what happened. Note these details of Christ's crucifixion there pictured.

(a). The very words that Christ uttered on the cross, "My God, my God, why hast thou forsaken me?" were

foretold in verse 1. Now read in Matthew 27: 46 where
Jesus said those very words!

(b). What the onlookers would say to Christ was also
prophesied. Psalm 22: 7, 8 says, "All they that see me
laugh me to scorn: they shoot out the lip, they shake the
head, saying, He trusted on the Lord that he would deliver him: let him deliver him, seeing he delighted in
him." That was fulfilled, for in Matthew 27: 43 we are
told that the chief priests, mocking Him, with the scribes
and elders, said, "He trusted in God; let him deliver him
now, if he will have him: for he said, I am the Son of
God."

(c). Psalm 22: 18 says, "They part my garments
among them, and cast lots upon my vesture." That was
written hundreds of years before Christ was born. Now
see how that prophecy was fulfilled. Matthew 27: 35
says, "And they crucified him, and parted his garments,
casting lots: that it might be fulfilled which was spoken
by the prophet, They parted my garments among them,
and upon my vesture did they cast lots."

(d). Psalm 22: 16 says, "They pierced my hands and
my feet." How clearly the prophet foretold the nailing
of Christ to the cross, centuries before!

6. The Coming Saviour, When Crucified, Must Be Given Gall and Vinegar

Psalm 69: 21 says, "They gave me also gall for my
meat; and in my thirst they gave me vinegar to drink."
The fulfillment, hundreds of years later, is given us in
Matthew 27: 33, 34, "And when they were come unto
a place called Golgotha, that is to say, a place of a skull,

They gave him vinegar to drink mingled with gall: and
when he had tasted thereof, he would not drink."

7. The Season, the Day of the Month, the Very Time of the Day When the Saviour Died, Were Foretold 1500 Years Ahead of Time!

Again we mention that the Passover lamb to be sacrificed, roasted with fire and eaten by every large family
in Israel (or by two smaller families) once a year, pictured Jesus Christ.   Here is a remarkable fact; this Passover feast was given to the children of Israel in Egypt
about fifteen hundred years before Christ, and there it
was said that in the first month of the year (Exod. 12:
2) on the fourteenth day of the month (Exod. 12: 6) and
"in the evening," the lamb should be slain each year. The
phrase in the Hebrew is even more definite, I understand,
"between the evenings," or midway between noon and
night.   Thus if the coming Saviour should be slain at
the time definitely pictured by millions of Passover lambs
which had been slain as typical of His death, then the
Saviour would die at midafternoon on the fourteenth
day of Nisan, in the midst of the Passover season!

Well, that is exactly what happened.   In the Passover season, Jesus ate a preliminary Passover meal with
His disciples, but did not eat the Passover lamb.   No
lamb is mentioned. The day Jesus died was "the preparation of the passover" (John 19: 14).   This preparation
day for the Passover feast ended at sundown and a new
day began; and John 19: 31 tells us that the Jews has-
tened to have the body of Jesus taken down before sundown!   For at sundown began the first great day of the

feast of unleavened bread, an annual sabbath when no servile work could be done (see Exod. 12: 15-18). Jesus died on the very day foretold in prophecy fifteen hundred years before; the day on which every Jewish family, for hundreds of year, had slain their Passover lamb.

And what time of the day was it when Jesus died? It was literally midafternoon, as Matthew 27: 46 says, "And about the ninth hour Jesus cried with a loud voice . . ." and then verse 50 just below says, "Jesus, when he had cried again with a loud voice, yielded up the ghost." By sun time, used by the Jews, there were twelve hours in the day, twelve hours in the night. The ninth hour was 3:00 p.m.; Jesus died exactly at the specified hour of the specified day of the specified year foretold in the Bible. A man must be deliberately unwilling to see the truth, must be among the "fools, and slow of heart to believe" (Luke 24: 25), if he is not astonished and convinced by this proof that the Bible is the inspired, infallible Word of God, and that Christ is the long-prophesied Son of God and Saviour.

8. *Even Judas' Betrayal of Christ for Thirty Pieces of Silver and His Tragic Death Were Foretold*

In Zechariah 11: 12, 13 is a strange portion of Scripture. In the midst of a highly figurative passage about Bands and Beauty is this definite prophecy; that the price of a certain man should be thirty pieces of silver, that then in the house of the Lord, the temple, these thirty pieces of silver should be cast to the potter.

"And I said unto them, If ye think good, give me my price; and if not, forbear. So they weighed for my price

thirty pieces of silver. And the Lord said unto me, Cast it unto the potter: a goodly price that I was prised at of them. And I took the thirty pieces of silver, and cast them to the potter in the house of the Lord."

This prophecy is about the Saviour Himself—that He should be betrayed for thirty pieces of silver by Judas Iscariot—and this was fulfilled as told in Matthew 26: 14, 15, as follows: "Then one of the twelve, called Judas Iscariot, went unto the chief priests, And said unto them, What will ye give me, and I will deliver him unto you? And they covenanted with him for thirty pieces of silver." Then later, when Judas had betrayed the Saviour and received the thirty pieces of silver, he returned to the temple, conscience-smitten, to return the bribe. When they would not have it, he threw down the money in the temple and went and hanged himself. Then the chief priests took the money and went and bought a potter's field in which to bury strangers. This account is given in Matthew 27, verses 3 to 8.

Psalm 41 is about David, but it is also a prophecy about the coming Saviour. Verse 9 says, "Yea, mine own familiar friend, in whom I trusted, which did eat of my bread, hath lifted up his heel against me." So Jesus, sitting at the last supper and knowing that Judas would betray Him, said as recorded in John 13: 18, 19: "I speak not of you all: I know whom I have chosen; but that the scripture may be fulfilled, He that eateth bread with me hath lifted up his heel against me. Now I tell you before it come, that, when it is come to pass, ye may believe that I am he."

Even the fact that Judas would lose his place as an

apostle and that another would be selected to carry on his work was prophesied in Psalm 69: 25, and Peter quoted that verse of Scripture about Judas when the apostles started to elect his successor, as recorded in Acts 1: 20.

Many other details of Christ's birth, life, death and resurrection were foretold, but here we have given enough to convince every honest heart.

In every detail Jesus died exactly as had been prophesied the Messiah should die in Old Testament prophecies written hundreds of years before! That could be no accident. Only a supernatural revelation from God could foretell hundreds of years ahead of time so many, many literal, accurate details without a single error. The Bible is God's infallible Word! Christ Jesus is God's own Son, our Saviour.

Chapter 5

THE RESURRECTION OF JESUS CHRIST

*"Moreover, brethren, I declare unto you the gospel
. . . how that Christ died for our sins according to the
scriptures; And that he was buried, and that he rose
again the third day according to the scriptures: And
that he was seen of Cephas, then of the twelve: After
that, he was seen of above five hundred brethren at once;
of whom the greater part remain unto this present, but
some are fallen asleep. After that, he was seen of James;
then of all the apostles. And last of all he was seen of
me also, as of one born out of due time."—I Cor. 15:
1, 3-8.*

*"And if Christ be not risen, then is our preaching vain,
and your faith is also vain. Yea, and we are found false
witnesses of God; because we have testified of God that
he raised up Christ: whom he raised not up, if so be
that the dead rise not. For if the dead rise not, then
is not Christ raised: And if Christ be not raised, your
faith is vain; ye are yet in your sins. Then they also
which are fallen asleep in Christ are perished. If in this
life only we have hope in Christ, we are of all men most
miserable. But now is Christ risen from the dead, and
become the firstfruits of them that slept."—I Cor. 15:
14-20.*

"To whom also he shewed himself alive after his pas-sion by many infallible proofs, being seen of them forty days, and speaking of the things pertaining to the king-dom of God."—Acts 1: 3.

"Therefore my heart is glad, and my glory rejoiceth: my flesh also shall rest in hope. For thou wilt not leave my soul in hell; neither wilt thou suffer thine Holy One to see corruption."—Psa. 16: 9, 10.

"For as Jonas was three days and three nights in the whale's belly; so shall the Son of man be three days and three nights in the heart of the earth."—Matt. 12: 40.

". . . and the third day he shall rise again."—Matt. 20: 19.

"I am he that liveth, and was dead; and, behold, I am alive for evermore, Amen; and have the keys of hell and of death."—Rev. 1: 18.

Jesus Christ is alive today! He was crucified and buried, and three days later He arose bodily from the grave. Joseph's new tomb, where Jesus had been buried, was left empty save for the burial garments. Jesus straightway appeared to hundreds of people. He ap-peared to Mary Magdalene and "the other Mary." He appeared to Peter, then to the rest of the twelve, then in Galilee to a great gathering of over five hundred Chris-tians. Then again James and all the apostles saw Him, and finally Paul himself saw Him on the road to Damas-cus. Forty days Jesus went among the disciples, teach-ing them, strengthening them. They felt of His body, handled the hands with the wounds in them, and were convinced. They saw Him eat and drink. He taught them and explained the Scriptures. Every doubt was brushed away by the evidence which the Bible calls "many infallible proofs" (Acts 1:3). The twelve saw Him ascend bodily to Heaven. Later He appeared to Paul on the road to Damascus. Later still He appeared to John the beloved on the isle of Patmos.

One could not find a record of a single New Testament Christian who doubted the personal, bodily resurrection of Jesus Christ. The Apostle's Creed affirms, "The third day he rose again from the dead."

The resurrection of Christ has thus been everywhere recognized as a cardinal doctrine of Christianity. The old Catholic church believed in the resurrection of Christ. The Roman Catholic church believes it firmly today. The Greek Catholic church has always declared it. All the historic Protestant creeds affirm the resurrection of Christ. Not one historic denomination claiming to be Christian has denied the resurrection of Christ, save Unitarians alone. Unitarians of course are not Christians, and intelligent leaders of Unitarianism do not claim to be specifically and exclusively Christian. They do not acknowledge Christ as God and so have not been historically recognized as Christian. Historic Christianity is based on the doctrine that Christ died for our sins and rose again bodily from the grave.

By the resurrection, of course, we mean the bodily resurrection. There is not any other kind of resurrection. Those who say that they believe in a spiritual resurrection are parrots quoting, without thinking, some deceiving infidel, or they themselves are willfully trying to deceive. No one ever taught that the spirit of Jesus was buried in Joseph's grave. No one ever taught that the spirit of Jesus died. The resurrection from the dead refers exclusively to the body. It was the body of Jesus that died, when He said, "Father, into thy hands I commend my spirit" (Luke 23: 46). It was the body that they anointed with spices and wrapped in linen, after they had taken it down from the cross. It was that body, with wounds in the hands and feet and a great hole in the side, which they laid in Joseph's tomb. It was that body that the soldiers guarded, with a great stone rolled against the door and sealed with a Roman seal. It was that body that rose from the dead. It is the talk of a thoughtless ignoramus that says, "I believe in a spiritual resurrection." The only kind of resurrection there is is a bodily resurrection. And the Bible teaches that Christ rose bodily from the grave.

Before His death Jesus said to the dying thief, "To day shalt thou be with me in paradise" (Luke 23: 43). Christ's spirit went at once to be with the heavenly Father. Only the body of Jesus was buried and only the body of Jesus could be resurrected. There is no resurrection except the bodily resurrection.

To deny the resurrection of Christ is to deny His deity. To deny the resurrection of Christ is to deny historic Christianity. To deny the resurrection of Christ is to deny the Bible. To deny the resurrection is to place one's self beside the infidels and scoffers. If Bob Ingersoll and Tom Paine were to join a church and put on clerical robes, yet believe and preach their infidelity, that would not make them Christians. So, infidels in the church today are not Christians. Those who deny the resurrection of Jesus Christ deny Christ and Christianity.

I. The Importance of Christ's Resurrection in the Christian Faith

It would be almost impossible to overestimate the importance of the Bible doctrine of the resurrection of Christ. Consider the evidence of its importance.

1. *The Resurrection of Christ Is Part of the Saving Gospel*

In I Corinthians 15:1-4 Paul, by divine inspiration, plainly tells us that the gospel "by which also ye are saved" is "that Christ died for our sins according to the Scriptures; And that he was buried, and that he rose again the third day according to the scriptures."

There are two elements in this "gospel," as stated here. First, Christ died. Second, He rose again from the dead the third day. But both of these things happened exactly "according to the scriptures." Both His death and His resurrection were in literal fulfillment of the Old Testament prophecies and types and promises.

Read the two introductory verses again in I Corinthians 15: 1, 2. "Moreover, brethren, I declare unto you the gospel which I preached unto you, which also ye have received, and wherein ye stand; By which also ye are saved, if ye keep in memory what I preached unto you, unless ye have believed in vain." This is the gospel which Paul preached, the gospel that penitent sinners believed and received, the gospel by which they were saved. Then verses 3 and 4, which were quoted above, follow, defining this gospel that Paul preached and by which people were saved.

Note the strange statement in I Corinthians 15: 2, saying that the Corinthians were saved by this gospel, "unless ye have believed in vain." That is explained by verse 14 in the same chapter where we are told, "And if Christ be not risen, then is our preaching vain, and your faith is also vain." That is, the gospel itself is a vain gospel unless Christ be risen from the dead. Any gospel without a resurrected Saviour is a vain gospel that could save nobody. Any such preaching is vain, says the Spirit, speaking through Paul.

And why is the resurrection a part of the gospel? The very nature of the gospel itself involves the resurrection. The gospel, the saving good news, is that Christ died for our sins, died according to the Scriptures, arose again the third day, according to the Scriptures. Christ died for our sins and rose for our justification. If Christ be now dead, He can save nobody. If Christ be now dead, and if the ashes of His decayed body are now scattered in some obscure tomb in Palestine, then the Scriptures are not true and there is no good news for sinners.

And one must believe the gospel in order to be saved. Faith in the Bible has two meanings. First, there is the acceptance of certain facts as true and, second, there is a dependence upon those facts for salvation. One who does not accept it as true that Christ arose from the dead cannot depend upon Him, with saving faith, for salvation.

Believing that Christ rose from the dead is a part of saving faith itself. This is made clear in Romans 10: 8, 9: "But what saith it? The word is nigh thee, even in thy mouth, and in thy heart: that is, the word of faith, which we preach; That if thou shalt confess with thy mouth the Lord Jesus, and shalt believe in thine heart that God hath raised him from the dead, thou shalt be saved."

The two simple elements of saving faith here are, first, confessing with the mouth the Lord Jesus; and second, believing in the heart that God hath raised Christ from the dead. Actually, of course, the confession with the mouth is simply an expression of faith in the heart, as the following verse (vs. 10) says that one who honestly trusts in Christ for salvation is saved. The confession with the mouth is simply the outward evidence of the inward faith. But to confess Christ with the mouth is not an evidence of saving faith, unless the one who so claims Christ believes in his heart honestly that Christ rose from the dead, and that therefore Christ is God come in human form, and now sits at the right hand of the Father, and therefore is able to save us from sin. One cannot have saving faith unless he believes that God raised up Jesus Christ from the dead!

Every person who ever exercised saving faith in Christ believed in the heart that God raised Him from the dead as the Scriptures declare. It may be that many have not understood the implications of the doctrine. It may be that many knew relatively little about the facts of the resurrection. But everyone who ever trusted Christ accepted what God said about raising His Son from the dead. One cannot be saved without believing that Jesus is what He claimed to be, what the Bible declares that He is—the dying, risen Saviour.

It is interesting to note from the words of Jesus Him-

self in John 8: 21, 24 that the deity of Christ must be
believed before one can have saving faith. After saying
that He was one with the Father, that He was the light
of the world, that He was from above while they were
from beneath, Jesus said, "I said therefore unto you,
that ye shall die in your sins: for if ye believe not that I
am he, ye shall die in your sins" (John 8: 24). One
could not believe in the deity of Christ without believing in His resurrection. The resurrection is the proof
of His deity. Those who have saving faith must base
it on the fact that Christ died and rose again according
to the Scriptures.

How wicked, then, the hand of one who would take
away the doctrine of the resurrection of Christ! He
would destroy the saving gospel. He would make it impossible for anyone to be saved who agrees with him
that Christ did not rise from the dead.

2. The Resurrection of Christ Was the Single Sign of His Deity

Some people believe that Christ's miracles proved His
deity. They believe that when Jesus healed the sick,
cured lepers, gave sight to the blind, raised the dead,
stilled the waters of the Sea of Galilee, that He was thus
demonstrating His deity. But Jesus never claimed that.
In fact, He again and again urged people not to tell of
some miracle which He wrought. Miracles did not prove
the deity of Christ. Moses, Joshua, Elijah, Elisha,
Peter, Paul, and others performed miracles by the power
of God. None of the miracles of Jesus were intended to
prove His deity. He helped the sick because He had

compassion on them. He raised Lazarus for the glory of God (John 11:4). He did not do it to prove His deity. Miracles prove that one is from God, but they proved that for the apostles, as they did for Christ.

No, the sign of Christ's deity is not simply that He worked miracles. The sign of Christ's deity is His resurrection from the dead. That is what He Himself expressly taught.

Jesus is quoted thus in Matthew 12:39, 40: "But he answered and said unto them, An evil and adulterous generation seeketh after a sign; and there shall no sign be given to it, but the sign of the prophet Jonas: For as Jonas was three days and three nights in the whale's belly; so shall the Son of man be three days and three nights in the heart of the earth." No sign was to be given concerning His deity except the miraculous sign that after being three days and nights in the earth, the grave, He would come forth as Jonah came forth from the belly of the great fish.

When Jesus was glorified on the Mount of Transfiguration, it was simply a preview of the glory that He would have after His resurrection. Hence, the three privileged disciples were commanded, "Tell the vision to no man, until the Son of man be risen again from the dead" (Matt. 17:9).

This truth, that the resurrection of Christ from the dead is the proof of His deity, is given again in Romans 1:3, 4. There Paul wrote by divine inspiration, "Concerning his Son Jesus Christ our Lord, which was made of the seed of David according to the flesh; And declared to be the Son of God with power, according to the spirit of holiness, by the resurrection from the dead." Jesus Christ was "declared to be the Son of God with power . . . by the resurrection from the dead."

Since the resurrection of Christ from the dead is the one miracle that proves His deity, we can understand why Romans 10: 9 says, "That if thou shalt confess with thy mouth the Lord Jesus, and shalt believe in thine heart that God hath raised him from the dead, thou shalt be saved." An acceptance of the deity of Christ is essential to saving faith, and the resurrection is the divine proof of His deity.

3. *The Old Testament Scriptures Plainly Foretold That Christ Should Rise From the Dead*

When two disciples walking down to Emmaus told the unrecognized Christ who walked beside them how that some women claimed that Jesus had been raised from the dead but that they did not believe, Jesus said to them: "O fools, and slow of heart to believe all that the prophets have spoken: Ought not Christ to have suffered these things, and to enter into his glory? And beginning at Moses and all the prophets, he expounded unto them in all the scriptures the things concerning himself" (Luke 24: 25-27).

Jesus meant that the Old Testament prophets foretold the death and resurrection of Christ; that the disciples were foolish not to believe the Scriptures and not to expect the resurrection of Christ. Then He showed them in all the Scriptures the things concerning Himself.

The clearest Old Testament prophecy about the resurrection of Christ is in Psalm 16: 9, 10, which says,

"Therefore my heart is glad, and my glory rejoiceth: my flesh also shall rest in hope. For thou wilt not leave my soul in hell; neither wilt thou suffer thine Holy One to see corruption."

This Scripture was used by Peter in Acts 2: 26, 27, in preaching at Pentecost on the resurrection of Christ. Here we have foretold in the Old Testament the feeling of Christ Himself, rejoicing that, when He should give up the ghost and lay His life down, His flesh would rest in hope, knowing that the Father would not leave His soul in death, and that His body would not see corruption, but would be raised from the grave. The body of Jesus was never to decay, was never to return to dust. That body had to be raised from the dead and then triumphantly the Lord Jesus later ascended to Heaven and that same Saviour with that same resurrected body is in the Glory-land now waiting for us.

It is quite clear to good Bible students that the story of Jonah's being swallowed by a whale (a great fish, the Scripture calls it) was given primarily as a type of the burial and resurrection of Christ. Jesus Himself said, "There shall no sign be given to it, but the sign of the prophet Jonas: For as Jonas was three days and three nights in the whale's belly; so shall the Son of man be three days and three nights in the heart of the earth" (Matt. 12: 39, 40). That Old Testament book of Jonah is meant to teach that Jesus would rise from the dead as Jonah was delivered from the whale.

I doubt if the average modernist and unbeliever in Christ even knows that Jesus expressly declared that Jonah's three days and nights in the belly of the whale was a type of His three days in the grave. But Satan, the enemy of our souls, knows it, and that is why Satan leads unbelievers to attack the Bible account of Jonah.

The Old Testament ceremony of bringing the first fruits of the crop to the Lord was evidently intended as a prophecy that the Saviour should be the first to rise from the dead. For I Corinthians 15: 20 says, "But now is Christ risen from the dead, and become the firstfruits of them that slept." Then verse 23 says, "But every man in his own order: Christ the firstfruits; afterward they that are Christ's at his coming." The Old Testament probably has many intimations of the future resurrection of Christ which have not been noticed by the average Bible reader.

For example, the second Psalm tells us that when the kings of the earth should set themselves against the Lord and His Christ (anointed), that "He that sitteth in the heavens shall laugh: the Lord shall have them in derision." And why would the Lord laugh when Herod and Pontius Pilate and the leaders of the Jews should agree to the crucifixion of Christ? Because, as the Psalm continues, God would yet "set my king upon my holy hill of Zion" (vs. 6). Christ, although crucified, is yet to reign over Israel. Then that necessarily involves the resurrection, though it is not specifically stated.

One of the clearest Old Testament implications of the resurrection of Christ is the Jewish priesthood, which of course was typical of Christ's priesthood. But how could the coming Messiah be both the sacrifice and the priest who offered the sacrifice? Only by rising from the dead after He died!

Melchizedek, mentioned in Genesis 14: 18 as "king of Salem" and "priest of the most high God," was particularly a type of the priesthood of Christ. Psalm 110: 4 says, "Thou art a priest for ever after the order of Melchizedek," referring to Christ; and Hebrews 5: 5, 6 tells us that these Scriptures and the type refer to Christ. Hebrews 7: 3 tells us that Melchizedek was especially suited to be a type of Christ, since the record of Melchizedek gives no father, no mother, no descendent, no beginning of days, nor end of life. These things were omitted from the Old Testament record of Melchizedek so that he would be a fit type of Christ, and Hebrews 7: 16 tells us that Christ is such a priest, "Who is made, not after the law of a carnal commandment, but after the power of an endless life." Only in having an endless life, not cut short by death, could Christ fulfil the type of Melchizedek, in His priesthood.

Thus the priesthood of the Old Testament, picturing Christ's priesthood, clearly implies His resurrection.

Throughout the Old Testament there is a double picture of Christ. He is pictured as the Man of sorrows, and acquainted with grief, the One whom it pleased the Lord to bruise, the One by whose stripes we are healed, the crucified Saviour, as pictured in Isaiah 53 and in Psalm 22. But He is pictured also as the seed of Abraham who is to inherit Palestine, as the seed of David, the branch from the root of Jesse, who is to sit on David's throne. How can it be true that the Messiah, the Saviour, is to be crucified, paying for our sins (as is prophesied in Isaiah 53) and yet be prophesied to rule over the whole world (as told in Isaiah, chapter 11)? The answer

to that is the resurrection from the dead. Jesus died,
but He arose again!

This is the divinely inspired interpretation given by
Peter in his sermon at Pentecost, recorded in Acts, chapter 2. There Peter says of David, "Therefore being a
prophet, and knowing that God had sworn with an oath
to him, that of the fruit of his loins, according to the
flesh, he would raise up Christ to sit on his throne; He
seeing this before spake of the resurrection of Christ,
that his soul was not left in hell, neither his flesh did
see corruption" (Acts 2: 30, 31). Every Old Testament
prophecy that Christ should sit on David's throne, that
Christ should rule the world, necessarily involves the
resurrection of Christ. So Peter says, by divine inspiration, that David foretold that God, "according to the
flesh," "would raise up Christ to sit on his throne."

Thus the resurrection of Christ is a fundamental doctrine everywhere implied and sometimes plainly declared
in the Old Testament.

4. *Jesus Himself Often Foretold His Coming Death on the Cross and His Resurrection*

Jesus knew that He was going to die for the sins of
the world. He often said so. Jesus likewise knew that
He would rise from the dead and repeatedly He foretold it.

Jesus foretold His resurrection when He referred to
Jonah after three days and nights coming forth from
the whale (Matt. 12: 39, 40).

In Matthew 20: 18, 19 Jesus told the twelve disciples,
"Behold, we go up to Jerusalem; and the Son of man

shall be betrayed unto the chief priests and unto the scribes, and they shall condemn him to death, And shall deliver him to the Gentiles to mock, and to scourge, and to crucify him: and the third day he shall rise again." Jesus knew the whole program. He, with the Father, had planned it before the world began. But that horrible tragedy of His crucifixion would have a happy ending; "And the third day he shall rise again"!

In Matthew 17: 9, on the Mount of Transfiguration, "Jesus charged them [the three favored disciples who saw His transfiguration], saying, Tell the vision to no man, until the Son of man be risen again from the dead." The rising from the dead was in His mind all the time, as the triumphant finale of the crucifixion.

In Luke 9: 22 Jesus straitly charged the disciples not to discuss Him as the Christ of God at the present, "Saying, The Son of man must suffer many things, and be rejected of the elders and chief priests and scribes, and be slain, and be raised the third day."

In John 10: 17, 18 Jesus plainly said that His crucifixion and His resurrection were His own plan. He said, "Therefore doth my Father love me, because I lay down my life, that I might take it again. No man taketh it from me, but I lay it down of myself. I have power to lay it down, and I have power to take it again. This commandment have I received of my Father."

The crucifixion and resurrection were inevitably connected in the mind of Christ and in His plan, just as they are connected in the gospel as preached by Paul and other Bible preachers.

If Christ's resurrection was of so great importance

in His own thinking and His own preaching it is preeminently important for the thinking of Christians today.

5. *Bible Preachers Continually Proclaimed the Resurrection of Christ*

Most Bible-believing preachers preach on the resurrection of Christ at Easter time, I hope. But how different was the plan of preachers in Bible times! If we read through the book of Acts, we will find that practically every time Peter and Paul and other Bible preachers preached, they spoke of the resurrection of Christ. Evidently the resurrection is of far more importance than we realize, and we would do well to follow the pattern of Bible preachers.

When Judas Iscariot, the unsaved apostle, went and hanged himself after betraying the Saviour, the eleven disciples forthwith met. They, led by the Spirit, must elect another apostle and that at once! Why? They must have another man, making twelve in all who had been with Christ from the baptism of John on to His resurrection. Acts 1: 21, 22 says, in the words of Peter, "Wherefore of these men which have companied with us all the time that the Lord Jesus went in and out among us, Beginning from the baptism of John, unto that same day that he was taken up from us, must one be ordained to be a witness with us of his resurrection." The primary plan was that these twelve men who had been with Jesus all of His public ministry and who were themselves eyewitnesses of His death and burial, and who had themselves seen Him after His resurrection, talked with Him, handled Him, should continually give a firsthand testimony that Christ was really risen from the dead.

In the second chapter of Acts, verses 24 to 36, thirteen verses are given in Peter's sermon to the resurrection of Christ!

In Acts 3: 14, 15 Peter, preaching to the multitude gathered in the temple when the lame man was healed, said, "But ye denied the Holy One and the Just, and desired a murderer to be granted unto you; And killed the Prince of life, whom God hath raised from the dead; whereof we are witnesses."

In the same chapter, Acts 3: 26, Peter in the same sermon mentions again the resurrection of Christ, saying, "Unto you first God, having raised up his Son Jesus, sent him to bless you, in turning away every one of you from his iniquities."

The apostles were often arrested. And what was the doctrine they always stressed which aroused the enmity of the leaders? It was the resurrection! Acts 4: 1, 2 says, "And as they spake unto the people, the priests, and the captain of the temple, and the Sadducees, came upon them, Being grieved that they taught the people, and preached through Jesus the resurrection from the dead."

Peter, called before the rulers of the Jews, was asked, "By what power, or by what name, have ye done this?" (that is, the healing of the lame man in the temple). Part of Peter's answer is given in Acts 4: 10, "Be it known unto you all, and to all the people of Israel, that by the name of Jesus Christ of Nazareth, whom ye crucified, whom God raised from the dead, even by him doth this man stand here before you whole." Peter could not preach about Jesus without mentioning His death and His resurrection. The resurrection is a part of the gospel, one of the facts which is the basis of saving faith.

In Acts 4: 31 we find that the apostles and their converts were again filled with the Holy Spirit and we are told that, "And with great power gave the apostles witness of the resurrection of the Lord Jesus" (Acts 4: 33). The apostles may not have been good preachers but they were good witnesses. They had seen the resurrected Saviour and they insisted on telling it everywhere, in jail and out of jail, before the common people and before the rulers. "With great power gave the apostles witness of the resurrection of the Lord Jesus." May God grant us to be faithful witnesses also of the resurrected Saviour whom we have met, and who has shown His power in our lives.

In Acts 5: 29, 30 we find that "Peter and the other apostles" faced the Sanhedrin boldly and said, "The God of our fathers raised up Jesus, whom ye slew and hanged on a tree." Then naturally they proceeded to say, "Him hath God exalted with his right hand to be a Prince and a Saviour, for to give repentance to Israel, and forgiveness of sins" (vs. 31).

Paul's preaching abounded, likewise, in references to the resurrection of Christ. In fact, Paul based all of his theology on the fact that Christ was risen from the dead, after dying for man's sins.

Paul and Barnabas on their first great missionary journey came to Antioch of Pisidia and there in the synagogue Paul preached a great sermon. Telling how Christ had been crucified, Paul then said: "And when they had fulfilled all that was written of him, they took him down from the tree, and laid him in a sepulchre. But God raised him from the dead" (Acts 13: 29, 30).

Then, to prove the resurrection, Paul quoted the second Psalm where it is said of Christ, "Thou art my Son; this day have I begotten thee"; and from the sixteenth Psalm, verse 10, ". . . neither wilt thou suffer thine Holy One to see corruption." Then in Acts 13: 37, in the same service he says, "But he, whom God raised again, saw no corruption." Then, with this background, he preached to them the forgiveness of sins by faith in this resurrected Saviour.

When Paul went to Athens, the center of culture of the world at that time, he preached to them the resurrection of Christ. Acts 17: 18 tells us, "Then certain philosophers of the Epicureans, and of the Stoicks, encountered him. And some said, What will this babbler say? other some, He seemeth to be a setter forth of strange gods: because he preached unto them Jesus, and the resurrection." It had already gotten out that Paul was a resurrection preacher! Then when Paul stood up to preach to them, calling them to worship the unknown God (unknown to their heathen minds, though they had an altar erected to him), Paul said, "And the times of this ignorance God winked at; but now commandeth all men every where to repent: Because he hath appointed a day, in the which he will judge the world in righteousness by that man whom he hath ordained; whereof he hath given assurance unto all men, in that he hath raised him from the dead" (Acts 17: 30, 31). Paul says that God commands all men everywhere to repent because Christ has been raised from the dead and that authenticates Him as the One who will judge the world. Therefore men should repent and trust Christ. He is the resurrected Saviour and therefore will be the judge.

And what was the reaction of the Athenians, wise in their own eyes? Verse 32 following says, "And when they heard of the resurrection of the dead, some mocked: and others said, We will hear thee again of this matter."

Paul's theme everywhere he went was the resurrection. When he was, after his arrest, brought before Felix he was allowed to speak for himself. Among other things he said, "But this I confess unto thee, that after the way which they call heresy, so worship I the God of my fathers, believing all things which are written in the law and in the prophets: And have hope toward God, which they themselves also allow, that there shall be a resurrection of the dead, both of the just and unjust" (Acts 24: 14, 15).

Then again in the same talk before Felix he tells how he had made an issue of the resurrection before the Sanhedrin and says, "Or else let these same here say, if they have found any evil doing in me, while I stood before the council, Except it be for this one voice, that I cried standing among them, Touching the resurrection of the dead I am called in question by you this day" (Acts 24: 20, 21).

After two years Festus took the place of Felix as governor, and King Agrippa with his wife Bernice came to Caesarea to visit with Festus. Festus did not know all about Paul but as he reported the matter to King

Agrippa he showed that the cardinal teaching of Paul he understood.

The Jews "had certain questions against him of their own superstition, and of one Jesus, which was dead, whom Paul affirmed to be alive" (Acts 25:19). Yes, dear old Paul, everywhere he went, affirmed that Jesus was alive!

So it came about that Paul was called in to speak before Agrippa and came at once to the great point; that Jesus who was crucified, dying for men's sins, had risen from the dead and was able to save all who trusted in Him! Dramatically before King Agrippa Paul said, "Why should it be thought a thing incredible with you, that God should raise the dead?" (Acts 26:8). And then Paul proceeded to tell of his own conversion—how, on the road to Damascus to punish Christians, he was struck down at midday and heard a voice speaking, and behold, it was the voice of this same resurrected Jesus! And there Paul saw the Saviour. Remember that in I Corinthians 15:8, after telling of all of the eyewitnesses of the Saviour's resurrection, Paul had said, "And last of all he was seen of me also, as of one born out of due time." Paul meant that one day all the remnant of Jews left alive will see the Saviour and that blind spiritual eyes will be opened and they will know Him and love Him and serve Him. But he, Paul, was born ahead of time, it seems, converted before the remnant of Jews. He himself saw Jesus. I think it was there on the road to Damascus. I think that is why Paul was struck blind. The glory of that face, that resurrected Jesus, struck Paul blind! I do not wonder that John, on the isle of Patmos, fell at his feet as one dead, when he saw Him, as he tells us in Revelation 1: 17. So Paul told King Agrippa of his personal acquaintance with the resurrected Saviour.

In that noble defense before King Agrippa, Paul gives again the substance of his whole gospel. In Acts 26:22, 23 he says, "Having therefore obtained help of God, I continue unto this day, witnessing both to small and great, saying none other things than those which the prophets and Moses did say should come: That Christ should suffer, and that he should be the first that should rise from the dead, and should shew light unto the people, and to the Gentiles." Paul preached, proving his points by many Old Testament Scriptures, that Christ was prophesied to suffer on the cross "and that he should be the first that should rise from the dead."

We can be sure from Paul's statement in I Corinthians 15: 3, 4 that the resurrection of Christ, according to the Scriptures, was part of the saving gospel he preached, and from the examples given in the book of Acts, that Paul everywhere preached the resurrection of Christ when he preached the gospel.

We can draw no other conclusion than that the resurrection is as vital a part of the gospel, as preached by New Testament preachers, as the death of Christ itself. Oh, then let us testify to the fact that Christ is risen from the dead!

6. *The Resurrection of Christ Is Essential Basis of Other Great Bible Doctrines*

We have shown above that the resurrection of Christ

was the single great proof of His deity and that belief in the resurrection is essential to saving faith, since the resurrection of Christ is part of the saving gospel itself, as taught in I Corinthians 15: 3, 4.

But there are certain other great doctrines of the Christian faith which are based upon the resurrection of Christ. Without the bodily resurrection of Christ, these essential facts could not be and these doctrines would be untenable.

First, Christ's resurrection from the dead was essential to our justification. The believer in Christ is justified, by which we mean that legally he is counted innocent and just. Christ was counted guilty for our sake. One who believes in Christ is counted just.

In Romans, chapter 4, we are clearly taught that "Abraham believed God, and it was counted unto him for righteousness" (vs. 3). And again, "It was imputed to him for righteousness" (vs. 22). Then Romans 4: 24, 25 says: "But for us also, to whom it shall be imputed, if we believe on him that raised up Jesus our Lord from the dead; Who was delivered for our offences, and was raised again for our justification."

Again the theme comes in that salvation of a sinner would be impossible if Christ had not risen from the dead. And one who believes in Christ must believe that He arose from the dead. God's raising Christ from the dead proved that He was willing to forgive sinners. Christ's rising from the dead proved that He was the Son of God and able to save. And if Christ died to pay for our sins (our offences, verse 25 calls them), He was raised from the dead for our justification. Christ, having died and risen again, is the perpetual witness that sin has been paid for. He can always present the wounds in His hands and His feet and the scar in His side to prove that the demands of the law have been fully met, that sin has been paid for and that the believing sinner has a right to be classed as just before God, for Christ's sake. The justification of a sinner depends upon Christ's resurrection.

In Romans 5: 10 this doctrine is reiterated. "For if, when we were enemies, we were reconciled to God by the death of his Son, much more, being reconciled, we shall be saved by his life." I think we might say that we were reconciled to God by the death of His Son but we are continually kept by His resurrected life.

Second, a kindred doctrine to our justification by the resurrection of Christ is the Bible truth that Christ's high-priestly intercession for us depended upon His resurrection from the dead. If Christ were to represent in Heaven before the Father those on earth who have trusted Him for salvation, He must be a living man, to represent living men. Christ died as a man and so Christ must rise as a man and live in Heaven as a man, to be man's mediator and priest.

This is clearly taught in Hebrews 7: 23-25 which says: "And they truly were many priests, because they were not suffered to continue by reason of death: But this man, because he continueth ever, hath an unchangeable priesthood. Wherefore he is able also to save them to the uttermost that come unto God by him, seeing he ever liveth to make intercession for them."

One trouble with the priests of the Old Testament times, priests of the first covenant, was that "they were not suffered to continue by reason of death." No human priest would be adequate to appear for men before God, if that priest should die and his priesthood end. But that is not the case with Jesus, as verse 24 explains. "But this man, because he continueth ever, hath an unchangeable priesthood."

Oh, thank God for the blessed teaching of verse 25 that Christ is able to save us to the uttermost that come to God by Him, "seeing he ever liveth to make intercession for them"!

One of the great essentials of a high priest in the heavenlies is that he must be one who "ever liveth." And Christ is such a living priest, risen from the dead.

It is a very shallow and inadequate conception of God's plan of salvation if we think that Christ died once and that henceforth He has nothing to do for the believer. Oh, but this very day He is at the right hand of the Father, taking the part of every sinner who trusts in Him. That is the reason that the Lord can keep all those He saves. In I John 2: 1, 2 is this blessed teaching. "My little children, these things write I unto you, that ye sin not. And if any man sin, we have an advocate with the Father, Jesus Christ the righteous: And he is the propitiation for our sins: and not for our's only, but also for the sins of the whole world."

We who have trusted in Christ "have an advocate with the Father, Jesus Christ the righteous." The living, resurrected Saviour is our mediator, our advocate, our lawyer at the court of Heaven! And this high-priestly intercession of Jesus depended upon His resurrection, as the Scripture expressly states.

A third great doctrine which is based upon the resurrection of Christ is the doctrine of a coming judgment. In John 5:22 Jesus tells us, "For the Father judgeth no man, but hath committed all judgment unto the Son." The reason given is that God wants "that all men should honour the Son, even as they honour the Father" (vs. 23). Christ is to be the judge whom all men must face.

Christians must give an account before Christ. Second Corinthians 5:10 says, "For we must all appear before the judgment seat of Christ." But primarily Christ must judge the unsaved world, must judge this world that hates Him, the world that crucified Him, the world that still rejects Him. That judgment the Father has committed into the hands of the Son. But it required a resurrected Saviour to judge those who crucified Him. So in his sermon at Athens, Paul says by divine inspiration, "Because he hath appointed a day, in the which he will judge the world in righteousness by that man whom he hath ordained: whereof he hath given assurance unto all men, in that he hath raised him from the dead" (Acts 17:31).

God has given all judgment to the Son. The proof that there will be a great final judgment is that Jesus Christ is risen from the dead! This living Christ, the Christ with a human body (the glorified and perfect One) on the great white throne—before Him shall be gathered all the unregenerate, and the record books shall be opened. Each one will be judged according to his works, by this risen Christ! The necessary basis for the coming judgment is the resurrection of Christ from the dead.

Another doctrine, very precious to me, which depends upon the resurrection of Christ, is the return of Christ and His reign on David's throne. God promised David in II Samuel 7: 16, "And thine house and thy kingdom shall be established for ever before thee: thy throne shall be established for ever." Isaiah 11: 1 tells how the kingly sprout shall come again from the stump of a tree (now cut down temporarily) of David's dynasty and how "a Branch shall grow out of his roots." That Branch, of course, is Christ in His second coming and reign. And the angel Gabriel, announcing the impending birth of the Saviour, said to Mary, "He shall be great, and shall be called the Son of the Highest: and the Lord God shall give unto him the throne of his father David: And he shall reign over the house of Jacob for ever; and of his kingdom there shall be no end" (Luke 1: 32, 33). Jesus is to have the throne of David and is to reign thereon personally, bodily. But that requires a resurrected Saviour.

That is what the Scripture plainly says. In Acts 2 Peter, preaching at Pentecost, quoted the sixteenth Psalm which promised the resurrection of Jesus, and said of David, "Therefore being a prophet, and knowing that God had sworn with an oath to him, that of the fruit of his loins, according to the flesh, he would raise up Christ to sit on his throne" (Acts 2: 30). God raised up Jesus according to the flesh, to sit on David's throne.

It is obvious that to believe in the literal coming and reign of Christ one must believe in His bodily resurrection. Dr. B. H. Carroll, the famous founder of Southwestern Baptist Theological Seminary at Fort

Worth and the most prominent theologian Southern Bap-
tists have ever produced, told Dr. W. B. Riley, shortly
before Dr. Carroll's death, that he had been greatly impressed with this fact: premillenialists do not turn out
to be modernists. Postmillenialists often did, Dr. Carroll
said. Yet Dr. Carroll himself had been widely known
as a postmillenialist, and his testimony is striking. I
use it here, however, wholly to illustrate the fact that
those who believe in the literal return of Christ and His
literal reign must believe in His resurrection.

Last, but certainly not least, the blessed hope that
Christians have of being called from the grave, of having bodies that never grow old, that are never sick, perfect bodies, glorified bodies, depends wholly on the
resurrection of Christ. The Bible repeatedly connects
the resurrection of Christ with the doctrine of the resurrection of others. In I Corinthians 15: 17-23 this
solemn and beautiful teaching is given.

*"17 And if Christ be not raised, your faith is vain; ye
are yet in your sins. 18 Then they also which are fallen
asleep in Christ are perished. 19 If in this life only we
have hope in Christ, we are of all men most miserable.
20 But now is Christ risen from the dead, and become the
firstfruits of them that slept. 21 For since by man came
death, by man came also the resurrection of the dead.
22 For as in Adam all die, even so in Christ shall all be
made alive. 23 But every man in his own order: Christ
the firstfruits; afterward they that are Christ's at his
coming."*

Verse 17 says that if Christ be not raised our faith
is vain and all of us who trusted in Him are still lost!

Verse 18 tells us that if Christ be not raised then all the Christians who have fallen asleep are perished, are gone forever, and we will never see them again. Small wonder that the next verse says that if in this life only we have hope in Christ "we are of all men most miserable"! But then comes the triumphant statement in verse 20, that Christ is now risen from the dead "and become the firstfruits of them that slept." Verse 23 says again that Christ is the firstfruits, and then afterward they that are Christ's at His coming. When Jesus comes He will raise the Christian dead and change the Christians that are living. And all this is guaranteed by His own resurrection from the dead.

This precious doctrine is taught again in Philippians 3: 20, 21 which says, "For our conversation is in heaven; from whence also we look for the Saviour, the Lord Jesus Christ: Who shall change our vile body, that it may be fashioned like unto his glorious body, according to the working whereby he is able even to subdue all things unto himself."

Here we are told that true Christians look happily for the coming of the Saviour, knowing that He "shall change our vile body, that it may be fashioned like unto his glorious body." If Christ, with a resurrected body, came out of Joseph's tomb and lives again, then thank God we will be changed and glorified and receive bodies like unto His glorious body, when He comes!

Again in Romans 8: 11 the Holy Spirit tells us that He who raised up Jesus from the dead will also raise up us, in whom the same Spirit dwells. "But if the Spirit of him that raised up Jesus from the dead dwell in you, he that raised up Christ from the dead shall also quicken your mortal bodies by his Spirit that dwelleth in you." Our resurrection depends on the resurrection of Christ. If He is risen then we, too, who trust in Him and in whom the Spirit makes His home, shall be raised from the dead, if we sleep; and shall be instantly changed and glorified if we are yet alive, when Jesus comes.

Any teaching that the body of Jesus decayed and mouldered in the dust in a Palestinian grave is not Christianity. Any body of doctrine that omits the personal, literal resurrection of Christ is not Christianity. It is a false religion; a pagan, ungodly religion. For this reason we must say that the modernist who denies the resurrection of Christ is not a Christian. He has denied the deity of Christ, for Jesus said that His deity would be proved by the one sign of His resurrection. He has denied the integrity of the Bible which everywhere, in the Old Testament and the New Testament, declares or implies the resurrection of Christ. He has turned his back on historic Christianity, the kind of Christianity preached by the apostles and held by saints and martyrs down through the centuries. Anybody who denies the basic fact of the resurrection of Christ has denied Christianity itself, has denied Christ, has denied the Bible, has denied the God of the Bible!

Oh, may this doctrine become blessed and real to our hearts! Too many have said the Apostles' Creed, quoting ". . . the third day he rose again from the dead," and yet their hearts have not entered into the joyful anticipation and the glorious blessing that is ours because Christ rose from the dead! I suggest, dear reader, that with humble hearts we rejoice and praise God for our living, resurrected Saviour.

His resurrection is part of the blessed gospel by which we are saved.

It is a necessary basis for our justification, for Christ's high-priestly intercession, for the judgment of sinners, for Christ's reign on earth, and for our own resurrection.

7. Baptism Was Given As a Perpetual Reminder That Christ Was Raised From the Dead!

Those who turn away from Bible Christianity do so deliberately, willfully. Our Saviour did not leave the great central doctrine of our faith in doubt, nor did He leave them so they could be forgotten by any honest heart. He gave the Last Supper to commemorate His death and said, "For as often as ye eat this bread, and drink this cup, ye do shew the Lord's death till he come" (as revealed to Paul, I Cor. 11:26). This oft-repeated ceremony reminds every believing child of God that the death of Christ for our sins is the basis of our salvation.

But remarkably enough, the Lord added another ordinance, commanded to be observed by every convert, which shows His bodily resurrection. That ordinance is baptism. Romans 6:4, 5 says: "Therefore we are buried with him by baptism into death: that like as Christ was raised up from the dead by the glory of the Father, even so we also should walk in newness of life. For if we have been planted together in the likeness of his death, we shall be also in the likeness of his resurrection." Every person who has been baptized, then, should have remembered that Christ's death and His resurrection alike are part of the saving gospel. The ordinance of baptism, as given in the Scriptures, should be carried out faithfully, not as a means of salvation, but as a testimony to the death and resurrection of Christ, which is the basis of all of our hope in Him.

Colossians 2: 12, 13 gives us the same teaching. "Buried with him in baptism, wherein also ye are risen with him through the faith of the operation of God, who hath raised him from the dead. And you, being dead in your sins and the uncircumcision of your flesh, hath he quickened together with him, having forgiven you all trespasses."

Note that baptism reminds a Christian that Christ rose from the dead. And here we find that baptism typifies not only that the Christian shall be raised from the grave, as Christ was, but that even now the Christian has entered into the resurrection life. The Christian is to count himself already alive from the dead. He is to count that, in Christ, he is a new creature, so is to strive to live as if he had attained to the resurrection. Of course, all of us still have our frailties, and all of us are still in this frail, carnal body which is doomed to die, but thanks be to God, we can look forward happily with victory in our hearts to the time when our bodies will be raised up, as was the body of Jesus. And the triumph and happiness in a Christian's life can only come because Christ rose from the dead.

If one comes to you preaching any other doctrine than this doctrine of Christ, II John 10, 11 commands us that such a one should not be received into your houses, and you should not bid him God speed. He is an enemy of the cross of Christ.   The atoning death of Christ for our sins and His resurrection from the grave for our justification are the twin doctrines of the gospel, the basis of saving faith, the basis of most of the great doctrines of the Bible.

Hold this teaching dear, then, and rejoice in the Lord that Christ is risen from the dead.   Let us have an Easter in our hearts every day in the year, knowing that our Saviour triumphed over death, Hell and the grave and is even now at the right hand of the Father making intercession for us.   And one day we will see Him, Jesus our Saviour, the God-man who died and rose from the grave. We will be able to put our fingers in the nail prints of his hands and feel the wound in his side, handling Him as did the apostles when He was alive, and rejoice in the physical evidence, as they did, that He arose from the grave.   Oh, resurrected Saviour!   Oh, blessed triumphant hope of the Christian!

II. "Many Infallible Proofs" of Christ's Resurrection

Praise God we can believe in the resurrection of Jesus Christ! This fundamental doctrine of Christianity has nothing to fear from honest investigation, from intelligent consideration. The facts are so overwhelming they have convinced millions of people. They will convince you, if you investigate the matter with an honest heart. The evidence is overwhelming.

Acts 1: 2, 3 says that Christ gave commandments unto

the apostles whom He had chosen, "To whom also he shewed himself alive after his passion by many infallible proofs, being seen of them forty days, and speaking of the things pertaining to the kingdom of God." The Bible claims that Jesus showed Himself alive, "by many infallible proofs." Any honest heart should consider those evidences which the Bible calls infallible.

The Lord Jesus Himself drew near and walked with two disciples on the road to Emmaus, the day of His resurrection from the dead. Their eyes were holden, and they did not know who He was. He asked them why they were so cast down, and they told Him that Jesus was dead. Some of the women had been to the tomb and said that they had seen a vision of angels who said Jesus was risen from the dead, but they did not believe it. To these doubters of His resurrection, on that resurrection day, Jesus said, "O fools, and slow of heart to believe all that the prophets have spoken: Ought not Christ to have suffered these things, and to enter into his glory?" (Luke 24: 25, 26). Then He began at Genesis and continuing with the other books of Moses and all the prophets, "he expounded unto them in all the scriptures the things concerning himself." Jesus, speaking particularly of His own resurrection, said that anyone is a fool and slow of heart to believe, if he does not accept the word of the Scriptures.

This one crowning evidence of the truth of Christianity is credible and reasonable, and the only people who do not believe it are those who have hearts which are, because of their own prejudice or desire, slow to believe the Bible, slow to listen to God's Word. Only bias, prejudice, or wicked attitude make people doubt the resurrection of Christ. We will consider some of this evidence. And the more you study it, the more you read the Bible, the more you see the effect of Bible Christianity in changing lives and hearts and society, the more you are bound to be impressed with infallible evidence that Christ rose from the dead.

Jesus said, "If any man willeth to do his will, he shall know of the teaching, whether it is of God, or whether I speak from myself" (John 7:17 R.V.). The same verse, in the new Confraternity translation of the New Testament by Catholic scholars says, "If anyone desires to do his will, he will know of the teaching whether it is from God, or whether I speak on my own authority." Anyone who really wants to know the truth about Christ and His resurrection will find out. God will help him to know the truth. The evidence will be overwhelming, if the heart attitude is right as one studies the matter.

1. *The Character and Person of Christ Make It Easy to Believe in His Resurrection*

The proven character of Christ makes His resurrection from the dead easy to believe. He claimed to be deity, one with the Father. In the books of Isaiah, Matthew, and Luke, very specific claim is made that He was born of a virgin, supernaturally conceived by the Holy Spirit. All the references to Christ in the Old Testament and the New presuppose that He is God incarnate, that He is the God-man. That such an one,

God come in the flesh, should prove His deity by rising
from the dead is sensible and believable. Those who do
not believe in Christ's deity started their unbelief far
earlier than that; they do not believe in Christ Himself.

Who is there in all human history like Christ? His
personality, His moral purity, His spiritual insight, His
overwhelming wisdom, set Him apart as the only one
of His kind. Jesus Christ is absolutely unique. When
we compare with Him Socrates, or Buddha, or Moham-
med, or Gandhi, or Lenin, or Shakespeare, or Napoleon,
or Washington, or Lincoln, or Roosevelt, we find that
there is no comparison. The sages, the intelligentsia, the
learned of the world are children beside His wisdom.
Their moral codes and systems are fragmentary and inadequate beside His sayings. The heroes of the world
have their faults and frailties and it is taken for granted
that Jesus Christ has neither fault nor frailty. He could
boldly challenge His critics, "Which of you convinceth
me of sin?" (John 8: 46). If Jesus Christ said He would
rise from the dead, then sensible people will believe it.

2. *The Bible Has Proven Itself Credible, so Its Account of the Resurrection Can Be Believed*

The inspiration of the Bible, the deity of Christ, and
Christ's bodily resurrection from the dead all stand or
fall together. If the Bible be true, then the resurrection
of Christ can be accepted by sensible people as a fact.
And, thank God, the evidence is overwhelming for the
authenticity and divine inspiration and infallibility of
the Bible.

Scientists in every field that touches the Bible and the statements the Bible makes are continually accumulating evidence that the Bible can be trusted. The Bible is scientifically accurate. Ten times in Genesis, chapter one, it is declared that animals and plants are to bring forth *after their kind*. That is, there will be variation within the species only. Scientists have never been able to break this rule. They have never seen any new species started. The Scripture says that "the life of the flesh is in the blood" (Lev. 17:11). And now all medical men agree, though 150 years ago they would have denied the statement or would have had no idea what it meant. The Scripture declares that the earth is hung out in space on nothing (Job 26:7), that it is round (Isaiah 40:22), and that it turns on its axis so that at the same instant, in varying parts of the earth, it is night, morning, midday (Luke 17:34-36).

The historical part of the Bible is fast proving itself true. Modernists and infidels delighted to say that in the days of Moses no one could read and write. Since the discovery of the Tel El Amarna tablets, all historians know that the guessers were wrong and the Bible is right. Scoffers said that the nation of Hittites discussed in detail in the Bible never really existed. But now extended inscriptions on stone and tablets have been deciphered in the Holy Land and elsewhere proving that the Hittites were a mighty race of people and a great nation. Historical and geographical details mentioned by the Bible are proving true more and more as the facts are discovered from profane sources. There really were two cities, Sodom and Gomorrah, destroyed by fire from heaven. Their ruins are under the Dead Sea and grave-yards have been found near the Dead Sea with the marks of fire and brimstone on the rocks. Historically and scientifically the Bible has proven itself to any honest investigating mind.

The prophetic predictions of the Bible have proven it supernaturally inspired. Scores of prophecies about the Saviour were fulfilled to the letter. He was born of a virgin, of the tribe of Judah, born in Bethlehem, exactly as prophesied. He was born at the very time foretold by Daniel 9:25. In His life, in His triumphal entry, in His betrayal by a friend, in His crucifixion, in His words on the cross, in His death on the very day foretold by fifteen hundred years of Passover lambs dying, He fulfilled the Scriptures. Sensible people cannot believe that all that was an accident. The second chapter of Daniel gives an outline of world history with the four great world empires, Babylon, Media-Persia, Greece, and Rome, and indicates the ten nations that would emerge from the broken Roman Empire. Any thoughtful man, familiar with these prophecies and with their fulfillment, is bound to believe the Bible.

I say that the fact that the Bible repeatedly states that Jesus rose from the dead and that this is one of the cen-tral tenets of Christianity, of Bible religion, predis-poses honest and openhearted people to believe in the resurrection, as they must believe other things taught in the Word of God, so long proven as credible.

3. *The Overwhelming Evidence of Christ's Resurrection Convinced All New Testament Christians*

The apostles were very practical men, not easy to deceive. Although Jesus told them again and again that He would rise from the dead, they did not understand or they simply could not believe the truth. There is no evidence that a single one of the New Testament Christians had much faith that Christ would rise from the dead. They were so set in their conviction that Christ was dead, permanently dead, that even when they saw Him many did not recognize Him at first. Mary thought He was the gardener. The two disciples on the road to Emmaus in Luke 24 did not recognize Him. The apostles did not first believe when the women told them that He was risen from the dead. Doubting Thomas did not believe the others of the eleven when they told him plainly that they had seen and talked with the risen Saviour. Mark 16: 9-13 discusses this unbelief of the disciples. "Now when Jesus was risen early the first day of the week, he appeared first to Mary Magdalene, out of whom he had cast seven devils. And she went and told them that had been with him, as they mourned and wept. And they, when they had heard that he was alive, and had been seen of her, believed not. After that he appeared in another form unto two of them, as they walked, and went into the country. And they went and told it unto the residue: neither believed they them."

The disciples did not believe Mary Magdalene. They did not believe those two who walked on the road to Emmaus and talked to Jesus. When Jesus sat with them He "upbraided them with their unbelief and hardness of heart, because they believed not them which had seen him after he was risen."

Even when the rest of the disciples were convinced that Jesus had really risen from the dead, because they had seen Him and talked with Him, Thomas did not believe. John 20: 24-29 tells of Christ's return visit a week later when the doubter was convinced. "But Thomas, one of the twelve, called Didymus, was not with them when Jesus came. The other disciples therefore said unto him, We have seen the Lord. But he said unto them, Except I shall see in his hands the print of the nails, and put my finger into the print of the nails, and thrust my hand into his side, I will not believe. And after eight days again his disciples were within, and Thomas with them: then came Jesus, the doors being shut, and stood in the midst, and said, Peace be unto you. Then saith he to Thomas, Reach hither thy finger, and behold my hands; and reach hither thy hand, and thrust it into my side: and be not faithless, but believing. And Thomas answered and said unto him, My Lord and my God. Jesus saith unto him, Thomas, because thou hast seen me, thou hast believed: blessed are they that have not seen, and yet have believed." Thomas was finally convinced. But he was first as stubborn an unbeliever as any honest man could well be.

Do not say that the disciples were gullible, that they were easily deceived. That is not true. Such a statement is foolish. All the evidence that an honest man could require, they did require. They would not believe that Jesus had risen from the dead until it was proven beyond the shadow of a doubt.

The evidence presented to the New Testament Christians was overwhelming. The worst doubter among them had to give up his doubts and accept it as a proven fact that Christ was risen from the dead.

There were some three thousand new converts added to the number of believers in Jerusalem on the day of Pentecost. Every one of them was convinced of the literal resurrection of Christ from the dead. That was the major theme of Peter's sermon to them. And thenceforth the New Testament preachers followed a regular pattern when they proclaimed that Jesus was risen from the dead. The apostles insisted that they themselves had seen Him alive, that they had put their hands upon Him, had seen Him eat and drink. When they worked miracles they declared it was by the power of the resurrected Christ. (For example, Acts 4: 10.) If they were filled with the Holy Ghost and mighty power, they explained it as a gift from the risen Saviour (Acts 2: 32, 33). Saul of Tarsus was convinced of the resurrection of Jesus Christ. So were all of the mighty Christians of his day. They declared that they knew personally the witnesses—above five hundred people had seen Him at one time after His resurrection, most of whom were still alive (I Cor. 15: 6).

The fact that the proof was overwhelming to the honest hearts who faced the evidence immediately following Christ's resurrection is conclusive. If you, any honest reader, had lived at Jerusalem and wanted to know the truth, you would have been convinced that Jesus was risen from the dead, just as all the others who wanted to know the truth believed it then. The fact that all New Testament Christians became convinced of Christ's resurrection, and most of them against their will, proves that the evidence is beyond question and incontrovertible.

4. What Were the 'Infallible Proofs' Which Convinced Everybody Who Investigated That Jesus Was Literally Risen From the Dead?

The Scripture says in Acts 1:3 that Jesus showed Himself alive after His passion "by many infallible proofs." What were these proofs, so conclusive, so compelling that every New Testament Christian was convinced, and that the truth could not successfully be gainsaid in that whole generation?

First of all, Jesus actually appeared alive, to the sight of multitudes. They saw Him face to face! First Corinthians 15:4-8 gives a long list of those who saw Him face to face, including one group of over five hundred people who saw Him at one time. Read it again.

"And that he was buried, and that he rose again the third day according to the scriptures: And that he was seen of Cephas, then of the twelve: After that, he was seen of above five hundred brethren at once: of whom the greater part remain unto this present, but some are fallen asleep. After that, he was seen of James; then of all the apostles. And last of all he was seen of me also, as of one born out of due time."

There is no hallucination here, no "vision." Too many honest, hardheaded sensible people saw Jesus Christ personally after His resurrection for it to be doubted.

Not only did the disciples see Jesus after His resurrection, but they put their hands upon Him, they felt of His body, they saw Him eat and drink before them. In Luke 24: 37-43 we have an account of how Jesus convinced the unbelieving disciples that it was really He, risen in the flesh.

"But they were terrified and affrighted, and supposed that they had seen a spirit. And he said unto them, Why are ye troubled? and why do thoughts arise in your hearts? Behold my hands and my feet, that it is I myself: handle me, and see; for a spirit hath not flesh and bones, as ye see me have. And when he had thus spoken, he shewed them his hands and his feet. And while they yet believed not for joy, and wondered, he said unto them, Have ye here any meat? And they gave him a piece of a broiled fish, and of an honeycomb. And he took it, and did eat before them."

It was not a ghost, a spirit, that appeared to the disciples! They saw His hands where the nails had torn them, and His feet, and felt the bones underneath. "A spirit hath not flesh and bones, as ye see me have," He said. Then further to prove that He was there, physically, literally before them, He called for food "and they gave him a piece of a broiled fish, and of an honeycomb." How fascinated and delighted they were to see Him pick the bones out of the broiled fish and eat it; they also saw Him eat the honeycomb, and lick the sweetness from His fingers! It was really Jesus, their own Saviour, the one they had seen and heard so often. He was really risen bodily from the dead! And they were convinced.

Poor doubting Thomas was not with the other disciples the day Jesus rose from the dead, and he declared that he would not believe—"Except I shall see in his hands the print of the nails, and put my finger into the print of the nails, and thrust my hand into his side, I will not believe" (John 20:25). But when Jesus appeared to the disciples, then He offered all the proof that Thomas wanted. "Then said he to Thomas, Reach hither thy finger, and behold my hands; and reach hither thy hand, and thrust it into my side: and be not faithless, but believing. And Thomas answered and said unto him, My Lord and my God" (John 20:27, 28).

Every honest inquirer, everyone who found it difficult to believe that Jesus had risen from the dead, had the proof presented to him.

There are other signs given by Jesus after His resurrection which are not recorded. For John 20:30, 31, following the account of how doubting Thomas was convinced of Christ's resurrection, tells us: "And many other signs truly did Jesus in the presence of his disciples, which are not written in this book: But these are written, that ye might believe that Jesus is the Christ, the Son of God; and that believing ye might have life through his name."

These signs and evidences presented by the Saviour are part of the proof of His deity, because they prove His resurrection, literally, from the dead. And these

evidences are written in the Bible that we may believe
that Jesus is the Christ, the Son of God, and believing
may have life through His name!

Yes, they were many "infallible proofs" by which
Jesus showed Himself alive after His passion. And Acts
1: 3 adds, "being seen of them forty days, and speaking
of the things pertaining to the kingdom of God."

Forty days this went on, Jesus appearing to His disciples, answering their questions, teaching them, giving them the Great Commission. Forty days it went
on, and the doubting and fearing were convinced beyond
any shadow of doubt. This was their own Saviour,
risen from the dead. Jesus was with them long enough
to explain to them all the principal Scriptures concerning
Himself. He was with them long enough to give detailed
instructions about taking the gospel to all the world.
Forty days He was among the disciples and talked to
them, and continually gave evidence of His bodily
resurrection.

Literally hundreds of Christians saw Jesus alive after
His resurrection. Over five hundred saw Him at one
time.

Peter could well say, "We have not followed cunningly
devised fables" (II Pet. 1: 16), and John could properly
boast that he only spoke of "That which was from the
beginning, which we have heard, which we have seen
with our eyes, which we have looked upon, and our
hands have handled, of the Word of life" (I John 1: 1).

Consider how overwhelming was that witness of literally hundreds of people who had seen Jesus after His

resurrection, some of them again and again and again
through a course of forty days' time! The Bible rule
was, "in the mouth of two or three witnesses." Here
were hundreds of witnesses. Many a man has been
condemned to death on the testimony of one or two
eyewitnesses.

Only twelve men are required to agree on the jury
to settle any important case. Here literally hundreds of
eyewitnesses agreed that Jesus arose from the dead.
Not one person ever appeared to say that they had seen
His dead body after the third day, nor to contradict
any of the evidence.

The testimony of those witnesses—eyewitnesses, witnesses who had handled the Saviour, touched Him, felt
the prints of the nails in His hands and feet, saw Him
eat, communed with Him forty days—that testimony
was stronger evidence than any case required before the
Supreme Court of the United States or before any other
court in the world. Any group of scientists with one-
tenth of that much evidence would accept as absolute
fact any matter so attested. The evidence is so overwhelming that only those who do not want to believe
and do not check the evidence reject it. No wonder that
the Bible declares that Jesus "showed himself alive after
his passion by many infallible proofs."

5. *The Arguments Against the Resurrection of Christ
Are Unbelievable and Silly and Obviously Biased*

For over nineteen hundred years wicked people, enemies of Christ and of the Bible and of Christianity, have

been trying with intense zeal to disprove the resurrection of Jesus Christ. An examination of these arguments of those who deny the resurrection of Christ is one of the strongest proofs that Jesus really did rise from the dead. Consider the following remarkable things about the infidels who deny the resurrection of Christ and their arguments:

(a) Consider who makes these arguments. The Jews who hated Jesus Christ and murdered Him were the first to deny His resurrection. Liars and murderers that they were, what honest person would believe their testimony, their unsupported word that Jesus did not rise from the dead? And down through the ages that is the kind of people who deny the resurrection of Christ. The wicked, the profane, the drunken, the ignorant, the haters of Christ and of God and of the Bible deny Christ's resurrection. Carl Marx denied Christ's resurrection. So did Adoph Hitler. So did Lenin and Stalin and Trotsky. So does the whole Communist party. The resurrection of Christ is denied in the tavern and the bawdyhouse. Infidels in the pulpit deny it, to be sure, and then favor godless atheism and Soviet Russia over the American way of life. Surely such people are not to be trusted, neither in their moral discernment nor their judgment.

Harry Emerson Fosdick denies the resurrection of Christ. But remember that he is not a Bible believer; he never worships Jesus; he takes the part of infidels. More than that, his judgment is not reliable. Remember that he, very shortly before the Pearl Harbor attack, boldly declared for pacifism, and against armament in America, saying that it was absurd to think that Japan would ever attack America. Who would risk his judgment? The people who deny the resurrection of Christ are not the people to believe on moral issues.

(b) The denials of Christ's resurrection have never been based on evidence, but always on prejudice. The bribed soldiers who guarded the tomb of Jesus said, "His disciples came by night, and stole him away while we slept." Well, if they slept, they could not tell who got the body. That testimony would not be received in any court as valid evidence. No man is a good witness to what takes place while he is asleep. Not a single person was ever found who declared that he had seen the body of Jesus after His third day in Joseph's tomb. Not a single Christian was ever found to confess that the apostles and other converts had conspired to pretend that Jesus had risen from the dead. Were these hundreds of people who said they saw Jesus alive all liars and deceivers? And would they go to their death for the lie? Such an idea is silly and unbelievable. Many an expedition has tried to find Joseph's tomb, and then to prove by chemical analysis that a body there decayed. (Though even that would not prove that the body of Jesus was the one which decayed there.) But they have never found the slightest evidence to substantiate any such theory. The reason some people do not believe in the resurrection of Jesus Christ is simply that they do not want to believe it, are determined not to believe it, despite the evidence.

(c) These suppositions invented by infidels who try to account for the apparent resurrection of Christ are silly. They are so silly and unconvincing that unbelievers themselves can never agree. They are always trying to find some new and, they hope, more plausible answer to the evidence that Christ rose from the dead. Every infidel, every modernist, has his own theory, but none of the theories satisfy even the infidels.

"His disciples came by night, and stole him away while we slept," said the soldiers. Then why did not the Jews find His body? They hated the Christians so much, and the Christian movement was doing them so much harm, that surely they did everything in their power to find the body of Jesus. That would have stopped Christianity at its source. They never found any such body, never claimed to. In fact, the leading Jews themselves did not believe that Christ's body had been stolen away. Many of the chief priests themselves were converted later and others, though convinced in their minds that Jesus was the Messiah, still hated Him, as lost sinners do today when they reject Him.

One theory says that Jesus did not really die on the cross but only swooned, and after some time in the grave he revived and came forth and appeared to His disciples. They treated Him and He was restored to health. Consider first that this is only a guess, without any evidence in the world for it. Then, it is not reasonable to suppose that Jesus could be alive after being taken down from the cross. For six hours He had hung there. Before the crucifixion He had been scourged with

a Roman cat-o'-nine-tails, which in itself sometimes produced death. Then when He gave up the ghost, openly
said, "Father, into thy hands I commend my spirit,"
everybody was convinced that He was dead. They thrust
a spear into His side and into His heart and there flowed
out blood and water. Still He hung there on the cross
until Joseph of Arimathaea could go to see Pilate, and
Pilate could be assured by the centurion that Jesus had
been some time dead. Then Joseph took the body down
from the cross. The body was wrapped in linen and
spices and left in the tomb. The centurion declared He
was dead. The soldiers believed Him dead. The Jewish
rulers themselves were convinced that He was dead.
Joseph of Arimathaea thought so. Mary His mother believed it. All the disciples believed that He had died.
Jesus Himself had declared again and again that He
would die on the cross. In view of the spear in His side
and witness of all the Old and New Testament, it is
foolish to suppose that Jesus did not actually die on the
cross.

Another theory of infidels is that the disciples had
hallucinations and visions and simply thought they saw
Jesus. But how strange that hundreds of people could
have the same vision! And how strange that Jesus should
appear to them again and again! And it is particularly
improbable that the disciples should have hallucinations
and think they saw Jesus alive when none of them ex-
pected Him to rise from the dead. All of them had to
be convinced, against their former convictions, that He
was really alive from the dead. And hallucinations do

not reappear again and again, day after day, to hundreds of people, for forty days, and always remain the same! And hallucinations do not eat and drink in the presence of people, as Jesus did! No, such a silly supposition cannot merit the support of intelligent people!

Other wicked people say that the disciples agreed, all of them, to lie about it and to say that they saw Jesus. But consider that these disciples were not liars. They were good people. Enemies of Jesus were haters and murderers and liars, but not these good men and women who were willing to die for the gospel and went everywhere preaching the Word. They gave up home and comforts and friends, they spared not their lives unto death in order to witness that Jesus rose from the dead. To believe that it was only a lie, and that every single one of them stayed with the lie until his death, is silly and unbelievable. Besides, believing a lie does not make drunkards sober, does not make harlots pure, does not make profane people holy. What the gospel did for New Testament Christians and what the gospel has done for millions down through the years could not be the result of a lie.

All the silly arguments of those who try to explain away the proof that Christ rose from the dead are not worthy of the credence of thoughtful people of the world.

The evidence that convinced all New Testament Christians and has convinced many millions of others since that time is enough to convince any earnest and honest person who is willing to do right and has his heart open to the truth of God.

6. *The One Best Way to Know That Jesus Is Alive Today Is to Try Him as Saviour!*

I do not say that wicked men who do not love the truth and do not plan to follow it will always be convinced of the deity of Christ. God turns people over to a reprobate mind that they may believe a lie and be damned, when they repeatedly and intentionally reject the light He gives. That is the clear teaching of Romans 1:21-32. Why should God reveal His truth to people who would not follow it if they had it? John 3:19-21 says, "And this is the condemnation, that light is come into the world, and men loved darkness rather than light, because their deeds were evil. For every one that doeth evil hateth the light, neither cometh to the light, lest his deeds should be reproved. But he that doeth truth cometh to the light, that his deeds may be made manifest, that they are wrought in God." The reason infidels and modernists are condemned is not because they *cannot* believe the truth, but rather because they *will not* believe the truth.

But those who want to know the truth and are willing to follow it can find the truth. If you want to know quickly and surely whether Jesus rose from the dead, whether He is the Saviour, God incarnate, whether the Bible is His Word and true, then set out to read the Bible carefully and prayerfully. Read the gospel of John. Pray as you read for God to give you light to understand His Word. Ask God to help you see the truth and to follow it. Make up your mind to love and obey the true God when you find Him, to accept Jesus Christ as your Saviour and Lord, just as soon as God will show you clearly that He is the Saviour. And coming with such an open heart you will find that God will meet you. You will find that God's sweet promise, "Draw nigh to God, and he will draw nigh to you," is true.

Try God out on His precious promises and see if the living Christ does not prove Himself to you. Thousands of answered prayers have proven to me that the Christ of the Bible lives today. I have risked my home, my happiness, my honor, my everything on His promises, and thank God He has proved Himself again and again. I *know* that Jesus is the resurrected living Lord. And you can know the same, too, if you seek God with all your heart.

Consider again these precious promises:

"If any man willeth to do his will, he shall know of the teaching, whether it is of God, or whether I speak from myself" (John 7: 17 R.V.).

"Then shall we know, if we follow on to know the Lord" (Hosea 6: 3).

"Draw nigh to God, and he will draw nigh to you" (James 4: 8).

"And ye shall seek me, and find me, when ye shall search for me with all your heart" (Jer. 29: 13).

There are truly "many infallible proofs" of the resurrection of Christ, and all who want to know may know for themselves that Christ is risen, yes, may know Him as Saviour too, and Lord!

Chapter 6

WHAT IS WRONG WITH A MODERNIST?

"Beloved, when I gave all diligence to write unto you of the common salvation, it was needful for me to write unto you, and exhort you that ye should earnestly contend for the faith which was once delivered unto the saints. For there are certain men crept in unawares, who were before of old ordained to this condemnation, ungodly men, turning the grace of our God into lasciviousness, and denying the only Lord God, and our Lord Jesus Christ."—Jude 3, 4.

"But there were false prophets also among the people, even as there shall be false teachers among you, who privily shall bring in damnable heresies, even denying the Lord that bought them and bring upon themselves swift destruction. And many shall follow their pernicious ways; by reason of whom the way of truth shall be evil spoken of. And through covetousness shall they with feigned words make merchandise of you: whose judgment now of a long time lingereth not, and their damnation slumbereth not."—II Pet. 2: 1-3.

"For such are false apostles, deceitful workers, transforming themselves into the apostles of Christ. And no marvel; for Satan himself is transformed into an angel of light. Therefore it is no great thing if his ministers

also be transformed as the ministers of righteousness; whose end shall be according to their works."—II Cor. 11: 13-15.

"Knowing this first, that there shall come in the last days scoffers, walking after their own lusts, And saying, Where is the promise of his coming? for since the fathers fell asleep, all things continue as they were from the beginning of the creation. For this they willingly are ignorant of, that by the word of God the heavens were of old, and the earth standing out of the water and in the water: Whereby the world that then was, being overflowed with water, perished."—II Pet. 3: 3-6.

"But though we, or an angel from heaven, preach any other gospel unto you than that which we have preached unto you, let him be accursed. As we said before, so say I now again, If any man preach any other gospel unto you than that ye have received, let him be accursed."
—Gal. 1: 8, 9.

"Whosoever transgresseth, and abideth not in the doctrine of Christ, hath not God. He that abideth in the doctrine of Christ, he hath both the Father and the Son. If there come any unto you, and bring not this doctrine, receive him not into your house, neither bid him God speed: For he that biddeth him God speed is partaker of his evil deeds."—II John 9-11.

The Bible has much to say about certain false teachers who were to appear from time to time among Christians. It is said in the Scriptures quoted above that they will have a different gospel from Paul, and are to be accursed of God. They creep in unawares, are ungodly men, "denying the only Lord God, and our Lord Jesus Christ." Because of these wicked men in the churches, it is necessary for us to "earnestly contend for the faith," says Jude by divine inspiration. We are not even to receive these men, who bring a different gospel, into our houses, not to support them even by bidding them "God speed."

These false teachers, says II Peter 2: 1-3, "privily shall bring in damnable heresies, even denying the Lord that bought them," that is, denying the deity and lordship of Christ and His atonement for our sins. Many shall follow these false teachers; they will by "feigned words," insincere and deceitful language, stay in the churches, pretending to be Christians for covetous reasons, 'making merchandise' of the people they deceive.

Yet these deceivers, these who pervert the gospel and deny the Bible and Christ, may appear as angels of light! They may appear to be most pious, may use Christian language to deceive, and will deceive many, says the Word of God.

Again and again the Bible warns against these wicked men, these false teachers with a false gospel contrary to the Bible, these deniers of Christ, these deceivers who, for the sake of gain, claim to be Christians and stay in the denominations and churches, though they may deny every fundamental of the historic Christian faith. To be indifferent here is to disobey Christ and the Bible and be deceived. No argument of "brotherly love," no fear of criticism should lead a Christian to compromise with these infidels, the wicked enemies of the gospel of Christ.

I. What We Mean by the Term "Modernist"

The false teaching we have been discussing is modernism; the false teachers so often warned against in the Bible are modernists. They are also called "theological liberals," or radicals. They are sometimes called Unitarians. Sometimes their leaders are called "higher critics." All these terms refer to people who deny the great historic doctrines of Christianity.

They deny that the Bible is infallibly inspired of God, that it is God's authoritative revelation, to be believed and obeyed in all points. They say it is *not* God's Word, though some of it may contain God's Word. They say it is a human book, full of mistakes, not to be accepted as God's perfect revelation.

Modernists deny that Christ is deity, God in human form, "the only begotten of the Father." They are Unitarians, which means that they believe there is one God, only one person in the Godhead. They do not believe in the Trinity, do not believe Jesus is God. They say He is a son of God only in the sense that we are all children of God. Hence they do not believe in the virgin birth of Christ nor His bodily resurrection, since both of these miracles are proof of Christ's deity.

Modernists, denying the authority of the Bible and its infallible inspiration, deny its God-given prophecies, deny all miracles, deny the Bible account of creation. They try to provide a natural explanation for all things, to avoid the supernatural, miraculous explanation. Hence modernists believe man came by evolution instead of by direct creation of God. They deny the miracles of

Christ and others recorded in the Bible. They deny even the miraculous new birth, regeneration. Modernists teach salvation by character, by good works, if they teach salvation at all.

Remember, modernism is a matter of doctrine, not a matter of how one lives. A modernist, or liberal, may be a total abstainer, an outwardly moral citizen; may even be a respected preacher. On the other hand, a drunkard or gambler may not be a modernist at all, but a believer in the truths of the Bible. Do not call any one a modernist because he is worldly. Worldliness is one thing; moderism is another. One may lead to the other, but they are not the same. Modernism is a denial of fundamental Bible doctrine.

These unbelievers who claim to be modernists mean that they do not accept the old historic truths of Christianity. Instead, they have new doctrines, based not upon the Bible as God's revelation to man, but based on man's reason and man's partial knowledge and man's preference. Modernism is a modern religion, not the historic Bible Christianity our fathers knew.

If you want to know whether any person is a modernist, ask and insist on an answer to these questions:

1. Is the Bible (as given in original manuscripts) the fully inspired and reliable Word of God? The modernist says NO; the Bible believer says YES.

2. Is Jesus Christ the virgin-born Son of God, bodily risen from the dead, as the Bible declares? Modernists say NO; Bible believers say YES.

3. Did Christ's death on the cross atone for sins so that the sinner may, by faith in His shed blood, be saved?

The modernist, the genuine modernist, says NO. The Bible believer says YES.

Some people who have genuinely been converted, born again, have been misled and deceived on some points by these modern infidels, but such deceived people who really love Christ and have trusted in His blood for salvation, are not true modernists in their hearts, I should say.

Modernists Admit That Modernism Is Not Historic Christianity

To make clear to all that the difference between modernism and the historic Bible faith of those who are fundamental or orthodox in doctrine is as great as we say, and that modernism is a new religion which is not Christianity, I quote here from *The Christian Century*. This magazine is certainly the leading exponent of the false religion, modernism, in America. In an editorial of January 3, 1924, it says:

"Christianity according to fundamentalism is one religion. Christianity according to modernism is another religion. Which is the true religion is the question that is to be settled in all probability by our generation for further generations.

"There is a clash here as profound and as grim as between Christianity and Confucianism. Amiable words cannot hide the differences. 'Blest be the tie' may be sung till doomsday, but it cannot bind these worlds together.

"The God of the fundamentalist is one God; the God of the modernist is another. The Christ of the fundamentalist is one Christ; the Christ of modernism is another. The Bible of fundamentalism is one Bible; the Bible of modernism is another. The church, the kingdom, the salvation, the consummation of all things—these are one thing to fundamentalists and another thing to modernists.

"Which God is the Christian God, which Christ is the Christian Christ, which Bible is the Christian Bible, which church, which kingdom, which salvation, which consummation are the Christian church, the Christian kingdom, the Christian salvation, the Christian consummation? The future will tell."

You see that modernism is not Bible Christianity, but a new religion made up by those who do not believe the Bible.

Now that we see what modernism in doctrine is, we are ready to learn what is wrong with modernism. We will learn by the Bible that the modernist

(1) Is an infidel, not a believer,

(2) Is a lost sinner, not a Christian,

(3) Is a fool, not the wise man he thinks,

(4) Is a hypocrite, not an honest seeker for truth,

(5) Is under a damning curse of God and of Christ.

II. The Modernist Is an Infidel, Not a Believer

Second Corinthians 6: 14, 15 says:

"Be ye not unequally yoked together with unbelievers: for what fellowship hath righteousness with unrighteousness? and what communion hath light with darkness? And what concord hath Christ with Belial? or what part hath he that believeth with an infidel?"

There is a vast difference between believers and infidels. Believers should not be yoked up with unbelievers, says the Word of God.

What a Believer Is

The purpose of the Bible, particularly the Gospel of John, is to reveal Christ as the Son of God and to make clear God's plan of salvation by believing in Christ. John 20: 31 says:

"But these are written, that ye might believe that Jesus is the Christ, the Son of God; and that believing ye might have life through his name."

You see that one has missed the whole point of the Bible, God's revelation, has missed the gospel and God's plan of salvation, if one does not "believe that Jesus is the Christ, the Son of God." And without the understanding and acceptance of this one great, central teaching of the Word of God, that Christ is the Son of God, one cannot depend upon Him and trust Him for salvation and be saved.

One who believes the Bible, believes that Christ is the Son of God and depends upon Him as his own personal Saviour, is a "believer" in the accepted Bible sense. One who does not believe the revelation of God concerning Jesus Christ, His Son, is an unbeliever, in the language of the Bible and in the language of historic Christianity. Such an unbeliever is an "infidel."

In I John 5: 9, 10 God again connects these two, the written Word, the Bible, and the living Word, Christ:

"If we receive the witness of men, the witness of God

is greater: for this is the witness of God which he hath testified of his Son. He that believeth on the Son of God hath the witness in himself: he that believeth not God hath made him a liar; because he believeth not the record that God gave of his Son."

No man believes in Christ, in the Bible sense, unless he believes the Bible. These two are inseparable. The Bible is God's miraculous revelation; Christ too is God's revelation, God revealed in the flesh. One who does not believe the record that God has given of His Son makes God a liar. He is an unbeliever, an infidel.

Definition of Infidel

Webster's Unabridged Dictionary defines infidel as follows:

"INFIDEL, n. 1. In respect of a given religion, one who is an unbeliever; a disbeliever; esp.: **α**. A non-Christian or one opposing the truth or authoritativeness of the Christian religion. . . . INFIDEL, in modern popular usage (for other senses, see defs.), is a term of reproach for one who avowedly denies the tenets of Christianity and the truth of the Scriptures."

Note the difference between an infidel and an atheist. The atheist says there is no God. The infidel may believe there is a God but he does not believe that the Bible is the infallible Word of God, does not believe that Christ is God's own Son incarnate, does not believe that men are saved by faith in the atoning blood of Christ.

Mohammedans believe there is a God, but they do not believe that Jesus is God's own Son, do not believe the gospel message about Christ.   Hence the Mohammedan is an infidel, and for many centuries the word "infidel" was used primarily of Mohammedans in all the writing and language of the crusades.

The orthodox Jew is an infidel.   He believes in God, even the God of the Old Testament.   But he does not believe that Christ is the Son of God, "the Lamb of God, which taketh away the sin of the world," and so of course does not believe the gospel of salvation by faith in His shed blood.

Heathen people are generally infidels.   They usually believe in a Supreme Being, so they could not be called atheists.   But they do not believe that Jesus Christ, God's Son, is come in the flesh; they do not believe He is the Saviour and they do not trust and accept Him as their own Saviour.   They do not believe the Bible as God's revelation of Christ and of the salvation offered through Him.   Heathen people thus are infidels.

Tom Paine wrote *The Age of Reason* to prove that the Bible was not true, said that Jesus was not the Son of God and that Christianity was a false religion.   He was an infidel.   He did not deny that there is a God, so he was not an atheist.   But he did deny that Jesus was God's only be-botten Son and he did deny the cardinal, central doctrines of historic Christianity based on the Bible.   He was an infidel.

Colonel Robert Ingersoll, who lectured on "The Mistakes of Moses" and made good money out of his infidel lectures, never denied that there is a God, so he was not an atheist.   He denied that Christ is the Son of God in any unique and supernatural way, denied that the Bible is the Word of God and denied the fundamental doctrines of historic Christianity as taught in the Bible. Ingersoll was frankly an infidel, that is, an unbeliever in Christ and the Bible.

Modernists Rank With Paine, Ingersoll, Mohammedans and Heathen as Infidels

Now all genuine modernists are infidels, unbelievers. They are not believers in the Bible, are not believers in the God of the Bible, are not believers in the historic doctrines of Christianity as taught in the Bible. The essential doctrines of the inspiration of the Scriptures; the deity of Christ; His virgin birth; His atoning death on the cross; His bodily resurrection; the fallen nature of mankind and man's need, yea, the absolute necessity for a new birth; the eternal punishment of the impenitent, Christ-rejecting sinner; everlasting blessedness of the redeemed—all these great doctrines have been believed down through the ages by all the great bodies who call themselves Christian, whether Roman Catholic, Greek Catholic, or Protestant. Believers accept the authority of the Bible, the deity of Jesus Christ, and the gospel of salvation through His blood. Unbelievers do not believe in the deity of Christ, do not believe in the authority of the Bible nor the historic doctrines of the Bible.

It is clear, then, that every genuine modernist is an infidel. The doctrine of a modernist is not Christian doctrine. His convictions are not Christian convictions. Modernists believe the same doctrines that Tom Paine and Bob Ingersoll preached. They often use exactly the same arguments and quote the same time-worn, alleged contradictions and mistakes of the Bible! Never count a modernist with believers. Modernists place themselves alongside all the other unbelievers who deny Jesus Christ, deny the authority of God's Word, deny the gospel of salvation as taught in the Bible.

The undying shame of the modernist is that for unholy, wicked, shameful reasons he tries to be counted with believers, he seeks position in the church of Jesus Christ whom he denies. He continually misrepresents himself and deceives the people to hold a position among the believers in Christ and the Bible and to have their support. Modernists are infidels; they are not Christian believers. Their doctrine is not Christian doctrine and their religion is not Christianity any more than Mohammedanism or any other heathen or pagan religion is Christianity.

III. Modernists Are Lost Sinners; Not Christians

Let me remind you again that both Christ and the Bible are called the Word of God. John 1: 1 says, "In the beginning was the Word, and the Word was with God, and the Word was God," and refers to Christ. Hebrews 4: 12 says, "For the word of God is quick, and powerful, and sharper than any twoedged sword . . ." and refers to the Bible, the Scriptures. These two— God's revelation in the Bible and God's revelation in His Son—are inseparably connected. If the Bible is not God's revelation, then Christ is not God's revelation.

We have practically no reliable historic knowledge about Jesus Christ except that given in the Scripture. So it turns out that one who does not believe the Bible does not believe that Christ is the only begotten Son of God, does not believe in His atoning death, and so cannot accept Christ with saving faith. A genuine modernist rejects the Bible and thus rejects the Christ of the Bible. Hence no genuine modernist is saved.

Jesus Said Modernists Should 'Die in Their Sins' Unsaved

We have the clear word of Jesus Christ that those who do not believe that He is what He claimed to be, the only begotten Son of God, one with the Father, should die in their sins, unsaved. Please read carefully John 8: 21-24:

"Then said Jesus again unto them, I go my way, and ye shall seek me, and shall die in your sins: whither I go, ye cannot come. Then said the Jews, Will he kill himself? because he saith, Whither I go, ye cannot come. And he said unto them, Ye are from beneath; I am from above: ye are of this world; I am not of this world. I said therefore unto you, that ye shall die in your sins: for if ye believe not that I am he, ye shall die in your sins."

Jesus said plainly that these Pharisees who rejected Him as God's Son and Saviour should die in their sins; that where He, Jesus, would go, they could not come. There is not a modernist in the land—however much he prates of "the Christian way of life"—who lives as clean as these Pharisees to whom Christ spoke. They

were meticulously careful in their moral lives. They
obeyed most carefully every requirement of the ceremonial law. They were moral, religious, prayerful. They
tithed, they prayed, they fasted. They were chaste, they
were upright. Yet to these modernists of His day Jesus
plainly said, "Ye are from beneath; I am from above."
In the same chapter, verse 44, Jesus said to them, "Ye
are of your father the devil, and the lusts of your father
ye will do." And Jesus said twice, in verses 21 and 24,
to these modernists, these Pharisees, that they should
die in their sins. "If ye believe not that I am he, ye shall
die in your sins." One who does not accept Christ as
what He claimed to be and what the Bible claimed Him
to be is from beneath, not from above; is not going to
Heaven but is going to Hell; is not a Christian but a lost
sinner. He is not a child of God but a child of the Devil,
Satan, according to Christ's own words.

A Personal Acceptance and Faith in Christ as Saviour the Only Way to Be Saved

Many, many times the Saviour declared that only by
faith in Him could a sinner be saved. One who puts his
dependence, his trust in Christ, relying on Him for forgiveness of his sins and salvation from Hell, is saved,
has everlasting life. One who does not so trust Christ
is condemned, lost, unsaved.

John 3: 16 says: "For God so loved the world, that
he gave his only begotten Son, that whosoever believeth
in him should not perish, but have everlasting life."

John 3: 18 says, "He that believeth on him is not
condemned: but he that believeth not is condemned al-

ready, because he hath not believed in the name of the only begotten Son of God."

John 3: 36 says, "He that believeth on the Son hath everlasting life: and he that believeth not the Son shall not see life; but the wrath of God abideth on him."

Paul and Silas preached at Antioch in Pisidia, "Be it known unto you therefore, men and brethren, that through this man is preached unto you the forgiveness of sins: And by him all that believe are justified from all things, from which ye could not be justified by the law of Moses (Acts 13: 38, 39).

Peter told Cornelius and his household that all the prophets were united in teaching "that through his name whosoever believeth in him shall receive remission of sins" (Acts 10: 43).

To the trembling jailer who inquired what he must do to be saved, Paul and Silas replied, "Believe on the Lord Jesus Christ, and thou shalt be saved" (Acts 16: 31). One who has personally trusted in Christ, risking Him, depending on Him for forgiveness and a new heart and salvation and everlasting life, is saved, is a Christian. One who does not so put his trust in Jesus as his own personal Saviour is condemned already and the wrath of God abideth on him. Such an unbeliever is not saved.

Now it is obvious that when the modernist says, "Jesus was only a man, not God incarnate; He was not born of a virgin as the Bible says He was; He did not work miracles; He did not rise from the grave; He did not make atonement for my sins by his death on the cross; He is not the Lamb of God that taketh away the sin of the world"; then he has not trusted Christ as his Saviour, and indeed *cannot* trust Christ as his Saviour while his wicked heart will not turn from his rejection of the truth. He does not believe that Jesus is what He claimed to be, does not believe that Christ can save him and hence certainly does not depend upon Christ and does not even want to trust Him as a personal Saviour. He may talk foolishly about following the example of Jesus; he may say that Jesus is his ideal or his leader, and may say that Jesus was the greatest man who ever lived. But the modernist who does not believe that Jesus is God's Son, does not believe in the gospel of salvation by faith in His atoning blood, is not himself saved.

All genuine modernists are unsaved sinners, not Christians. All genuine modernists are Christ-rejecting sinners, under condemnation, with the wrath of God upon them, headed for the lake of fire.

The Modernist's Culture Cannot Give Him a Christian Heart

A minister talked to me with deepest agitation about himself and his ministry. He had a bachelor of divinity degree from Yale University, but he said, "No man ever had so fine a degree which meant so little. They taught us to turn a pretty phrase; they taught us nice orders of service. We grew practiced in the forms of worship. But we were not taught the Bible, we were not taught how to get men saved, we were not taught to know Christ." What a pity to be educated for the ministry but not even to know Christ as Saviour!

The modernist may have Chesterfieldian manners, and often has. He may be suave, he may be kindly, he may be humanitarian and generous. He may be a loyal friend, a conscientious and moral husband and father. The modernist may be cultured and intelligent, admirable in a thousand ways. But he is not a Christian; he is a lost sinner, an unconverted, unforgiven, Christ-rejecting sinner who is headed for Hell. His heart, by his own choice, stays unregenerate and wicked, turned away from Christ.

Oh, if some modernist reads this, I beseech you in Christ's stead to turn from your self-conceit, your intellectual pride, your rejection of Christ. You are not saved! You are not a Christian! You are in mortal danger. In Christ's name I beg you to repent of your sins, turn from your infidel folly and accept Christ as your own personal Saviour. When your wicked, proud heart repents, God will lift the darkness from your unbelieving mind and you will be a modernist no longer.

The worst thing wrong with the modernist is his unregenerate, carnal heart which has never been changed by God's miracle of regeneration. The modernist should not be argued with as a brother Christian but he should be preached to as a wicked, Christ-rejecting sinner. What is wrong with the modernist is more with his Christ-rejecting heart than with his mistaught and scornful head.

IV. The Modernist, the Bible Says, Is a Fool

The modernist is a fool, not the wise man he claims.

The Scripture says, "The wisdom of this world is foolishness with God" (I Cor. 3:19). In nothing is this more manifest than in the case of the modernists who do not believe the Bible. They leap to conclusions that the Bible is false and inaccurate without sufficient evidence. They follow atheists, not historic Christian leaders. They follow the foolish guesswork and suppositions of "science falsely so-called." They turn their backs on the faith of historic Christianity which has transformed the lives of millions, which has comforted and given peace and strength to every person who ever tried it. They renounce the salvation of God as revealed in God's holy Word and have followed the vain panaceas of ungodly, unbelieving men. Thus the modernist is not a wise man, but a fool.

Jesus Said Anyone 'Slow to Believe' the Bible Is a Fool

That is exactly what Jesus Christ Himself called those who did not believe the Scriptures. After His resurrection, Jesus walked on the road to Emmaus with two doubting disciples whose unbelieving eyes were holden that they did not recognize Him as the risen Saviour. To them He said, "O fools, and slow of heart to believe all that the prophets have spoken: Ought not Christ to have suffered these things, and to enter into his glory?" (Luke 24:25, 26).

And the next verse, verse 27, tells us, "And beginning at Moses and all the prophets, he expounded unto them in all the scriptures the things concerning himself."

Here Jesus expressly says that one who is even slow

to believe all the Scriptures have spoken is a fool. Not only is he a fool in his intelligence, making a silly mistake, coming to wrong conclusions, but he is a fool in his heart, with wrong attitudes and motives. When Jesus says, "O fools, and slow of heart to believe all that the prophets have spoken," He includes every modernist, every unbeliever in any part of the Old Testament.

Yes, Jesus had in mind all the Old Testament, for the same passage says that He began at Moses (the Pentateuch) and all the prophets and expounded unto them in all the Scriptures the things concerning Himself (Luke 24: 27).

To doubt the Genesis account of creation, as given by divine inspiration to Moses, proves one a fool, says Jesus Christ! To doubt the historical account of the great fish God prepared to swallow Jonah, and God's deliverance of Jonah after three days, as given by the prophet Jonah under divine inspiration, proves a man a fool, according to Jesus Christ!

But if one is a fool not to believe the Old Testament, he is a fool not to believe the New Testament, too. The Old Testament foretold the virgin birth of Christ (Isa. 7: 14), as the fact is recorded in the New Testament. The Old Testament foretold the bodily resurrection of Christ (Psa. 16: 10), as certainly as the fact is recorded in the New Testament. The New Testament is Scripture, and the New Testament writers were prophets in the very sense that Jesus used these terms.

Thus the Lord Jesus Christ Himself plainly said that every modernist, everyone who doubts part of the Bible,

is a fool! The conclusions of the modernist are not
intelligent. His judgment cannot be trusted. His
sources are unreliable. The modernist, or any unbeliever in the Bible, is a silly fool.

The Scientific Accuracy of the Bible Proves Its Supernatural Origin

The Bible commends itself to intelligent people and
any honest investigation assumes that the Bible is truly
the supernatural revelation from God which it claims to
be.

For example, Isaiah 40:22 teaches that the world is
round. Job 26:7 says that God "hangeth the earth
upon nothing." The book of Job, probably the oldest
book of our Bible, written at least 3,500 years ago, says
that God hangs the earth out in space, on nothing! This
accurate discussion of the nature of our planet was given
long before there was a telescope, before Galileo or Ma-
gellan ever thought the world was round, and when the
Babylonians, the scientists of the day, thought that the
earth was flat and supported on the back of a giant elephant, and that elephant on a succession of giant turtles!
The scientific accuracy of the Bible proves its supernatural inspiration.

Leviticus 17:11 says that "the life of the flesh is in
the blood."

Less than two hundred years ago Harvey discovered
the circulation of the blood, and only in the last twenty-
five years has medical science come to realize how definitely all the life processes depend on the blood. A physician
killed President George Washington by draining away

his blood when he had pneumonia. All doctors now know that the life of the flesh is in the blood. The absorption and distribution of oxygen, the elimination of carbon dioxide, the resistance to germ infection, the repair of tissues, the reuniting of broken bones, the growth of the body, its health and functions, all depend upon the blood. This absolutely scientific conception of the blood written 3,500 years ago, when human learning had not even dreamed of such a thing, proves that the Bible is the Word of God. Only fools could doubt it, fools who do not check up on the facts.

Bible Prophecies, Fulfilled Exactly, Prove Bible Is God's Revelation

The fulfillment of prophecies would convince every intelligent, honest investigator of the truth of Scripture. For example, Daniel 2 foretells the four great world empires: Babylon, Media-Persia, Greece and Rome. The same chapter expressly foretells the breaking up of the Roman empire into ten kingdoms, and this prophecy is fulfilled to the letter. Both the Prophet Daniel and the book of Revelation in the New Testament show that there will never be another world empire until the Antichrist, the Man of Sin, appears to restore in a brief, terrible reign the dictatorship of the last empire, Rome. How would the Bible writers know that neither Genghis Khan, nor Charlemagne, nor Kaiser Wilhelm, nor Hitler, nor Josef Stalin would attain their ambitions for world rule? They knew by divine revelation! Such prophetic exactness could not be accidental, and only a fool would not be impressed by it—the kind of fool who does not check up on the Bible to see whether it is true or not before he discards it.

How can one ignore the fulfillment of countless prophecies about Jesus Christ; His coming 483 years after the decree to re-establish Jerusalem during the captivity years (Daniel 9: 25); His birth of a virgin, of the tribe of Judah, of the lineage of David, in Bethlehem; His crucifixion on the fourteenth day of Nisan foretold in detail fifteen hundred years before; and countless other details? How can one ignore such evidence of the reliability of the Bible and the deity of Christ? By being a fool who does not face the facts!

Some Silly Mistakes of Modernist Fools

For the folly of modernists one could find a thousand illustrations. A few weeks before Pearl Harbor, Dr. Harry Emerson Fosdick was still crying loudly that Japan would never attack us, that we were foolish to arm against Japan, as already mentioned. The conclusions of modernists are not intelligent conclusions.

Modernists generally have been pacifists, declaring that mankind has become so cultured, has evolved so far, that future wars can all be avoided. Again and again the facts have proved them fools.

Modernists generally have been hoodwinked by Red propaganda. They have been easily deceived into thinking that Russia is a land of freedom and democracy, and some have even said that Russia, with her communism, was putting on an exhibition of practical Christianity! I am not speaking now of atheists who say there is no God, of irreligious men; I am speaking about men who are ordained as ministers, who claim to be Christians but do not believe the Bible; men like Bishop McConnell, Dr. E. Stanley Jones, Bishop Oxnam, the Dean of Canterbury, and other Federal Council of Churches leaders, professors in modernistic, liberal seminaries and liberal leaders in the denominations. A man who thinks communism is Christian, and Russia a democracy, is a fool!

Modernists who deny the Bible have been deceived by the silliest hoaxes for years. With other unbelievers, they accepted the story of the "Nebraska man," supposedly millions of years old, a prehistoric "missing link," conjured out of the imagination of the scientists from one tooth found in Nebraska by a scientist, Harold Cook. Then the rest of the skeleton was found, and it turned out to be, not a man, but a wild pig! Very smart, eh? Plaster models created out of the imagination and a few bone fragments picked up over a wide area form museum displays of so-called prehistoric men. And modernists point to these plaster cast works of art as evidence of man's descent from ape-like creatures! They are fools, easily deceived because they want to be deceived.

Modernists said there was no Hittite nation, mentioned many times in the Bible but nowhere else in literature. Now many inscriptions have been deciphered which prove the Hittites were a nation rivaling Egypt. A man is an ignoramus, a fool, to bet against the Bible!

Modernists scoffed at the New Testament because it was not written in classical Greek like Homer. Now it has been long proved that *koine* Greek, like that of the New Testament, was the kind of Greek commonly spoken everywhere in New Testament times.

Once modernists said that Moses could not have
written the Pentateuch because writing was not known
in the days of Moses! Now informed scholars who
want to know the truth know of the library of Amen-
hetep the Third, and the Tel el Amarna tablets and other
proof that writing was very common in Egypt long before Moses. And records of Ur of the Chaldees show
that there was much writing even centuries before Abraham. Any man who, in his ignorance, announces that
writing was unknown in the days when Moses is claimed
to have written the Pentateuch, is a fool. And now even
unconverted scholars know how silly such a man is.

Modernists are deceived, they come to unintelligent
conclusions, they hold untenable positions, they are not
trustworthy guides. They are not scholarly, unbiased
thinkers. Modernists, in the language of Jesus Christ,
are fools, not the wise men they claim to be.

Romans 1: 22 says of such, "Professing themselves
to be wise, they became fools." Romans 1: 28 adds
further, "And even as they did not like to retain God
in their knowledge, God gave them over to a reprobate
mind . . . ." All those who deny the Bible, deny historic Christianity, deny the deity, virgin birth, atoning
death and bodily resurrection of Christ our Lord do it
because their foolish minds have been darkened and God
has turned them over to a reprobate mind because of
their sins. Claiming to be wise, they have become fools.

Never defer to a modernist as if he were a wise man.
However cultured and educated he is, he has a perverted
mind and a darkened heart, and cannot understand the
truth. He is, in Bible language, a fool, not a wise man.

V. The Modernist Is an Insincere Hypocrite, Not an Honest Doubter

Jesus said in Matthew 7:15, "Beware of false prophets, which come to you in sheep's clothing, but inwardly they are ravening wolves." He warned us that some men would come who would pretend to be prophets of God but would actually be false prophets. They would pretend to be sheep and would come in sheep's clothing, that is, with the outward appearance of Christianity, but inwardly they would be "ravening wolves."

Modernists Are 'Wolves in Sheep's Clothing,' Are "False Prophets," Bible Says

Whom would Jesus call false prophets, wolves in sheep's clothing? The modernists! Those who do not believe in Him as the only Saviour, the strait way to Heaven. For that is the subject He discusses in verses 13 and 14 of the same seventh chapter of Matthew. Anyone who does not believe in salvation by faith in the atoning death of Christ is a false prophet, a wolf in sheep's clothing, if he pretends at all to be a Christian or a Christian teacher or minister. And in the following verses Jesus plainly says that such false teachers who pretend to prophesy in His name shall not enter the kingdom of Heaven. And in verse 24 He says, "Therefore whosoever heareth these sayings of mine, and doeth them" will be a wise man; and verse 26 says that anyone who will not hear the words of the Lord Jesus as God's truth must be called a foolish man. And the last verse in the chapter tells us, "For he taught them as one having authority, and not as the scribes." In reading that entire passage, Matthew 7: 13-29, it is clear that these wolves in sheep's clothing, these pretended Christian leaders who actually serve Satan, these hypocrites who are really false prophets, not true prophets of God, are those who do not accept the Christ of the Bible and God's revealed Word.

Does some modernist tell us that he is simply an honest, scientific student and that his learning compels him to doubt the Word of God? Do not believe him! He is an insincere hypocrite. He has not made an unbiased investigation. He has not wholeheartedly sought the Word of God. His motives are not pure, honest motives. His language is not honest language.

Modernists Bring in Damnable Heresies "Privily," With "Feigned Words"

The modernism of apostate teachers, false prophets, is foretold frequently in the Word of God. Second Peter 2: 1-3 pictures modernists in these words:

"But there were false prophets also among the people, even as there shall be false teachers among you, who privily shall bring in damnable heresies, even denying the Lord that bought them and bring upon themselves swift destruction. And many shall follow their pernicious ways; by reason of whom the way of truth shall be evil spoken of. And through covetousness shall they with feigned words make merchandise of you: whose judgment now of a long time lingereth not, and their damnation slumbereth not."

Verse 1, quoted above, shows that God had modernists

in mind, "who privily shall bring in damnable heresies, even denying the Lord that bought them." Such pretended Christians turn away from historic Christianity and so their doctrines are heresies, untrue to the Word of God. And all who deny the inspiration of the Bible also deny "the Lord that bought them." The integrity of the Bible as the infallible Word of God and the deity and atoning death of Christ stand or fall together. Those who deny the one generally deny the other. And one who denies either the Word of God or the deity of Christ is a modernist.

Now notice that the Scripture says these modernists are insincere hypocrites. First, they bring in "damnable heresies" *privily*, says verse 1. Modernists do not come out and say honestly and frankly, "I am an infidel. I agree with Voltaire, Renan, Tom Paine, Robert Ingersoll. I am not a Christian in the honest acceptance of the term as used for nineteen centuries." No, a modernist infidel claims to be a Christian, often takes ordination vows to defend the Bible and preach the gospel, though privately he does not mean to do it. The modernist is a fifth columnist in the church, privily bringing in damnable heresies, as the Scripture says. That is not an honest position. It is the position of a hypocrite. Second Peter 2:3 explains further why these false prophets, modernists, come in so privily. "And through covetousness shall they with feigned words make merchandise of you." The modernist's words are "feigned words," insincere words. If he says he believes in the inspiration of the Bible, he does not mean by the word "inspiration" what honest people have meant through the centuries,

that it is God-breathed revelation. He simply means it
is a very nice piece of literature, like Tennyson's poems
or Shakespeare's plays. If a modernist says Christ is
the Son of God, he is using Christian language, but he
does not mean Christian truth. He simply means that all
men, regenerate or unregenerate, are alike the sons of
God and that Jesus is like other men!

Modernists Intentionally Use Deceitful Language, Take Vows They Intend to Break

In Dr. Harry Emerson Fosdick's book, *The Hope of
the World,* he has a sermon on "The Peril of Worshiping
Jesus" which is a model of insincerity and hypocrisy.
Though Jesus Himself openly declared, "Hereafter shall
ye see the Son of man sitting on the right hand of power,
and coming in the clouds of heaven" (Matt. 26: 64),
and said, "I and my Father are one" (John 10: 30),
and claimed that He was the "I AM" before Abraham
and that the Father had given all judgment to the Son;
yet Fosdick blasphemously pretends that Jesus did not
want to be worshipped. In the same sermon this noted
modernist says that certainly Jesus was divine, even as
Fosdick's mother was divine! Such language is insincere, hypocritical language. Such words are feigned
words, as the Scripture expressly declares modernists
would use.

When a modernist speaks of Christianity, he does not
mean Bible Christianity. When a modernist speaks of
the gospel, he does not mean the gospel of salvation by
the blood of Christ, taught in the Word of God. He
does not mean the gospel which Paul preached, "how

that Christ died for our sins according to the scriptures: And that he was buried, and that he rose again the third day according to the scriptures" (I Cor. 15: 3, 4).

When a modernist agrees to defend the orthodox "Articles of Religion" of the Methodist church, or when he takes a vow that he will uphold the Westminster Confession of Faith and the historic doctrine of the Presbyterian church, and does not do it, he is a lying hypocrite, not worthy of the respect of honest people anywhere.

But let us look again to the Word of God, to find the motives back of the insincerity and "feigned words" of the modernist. Second Peter 2: 3 says, "And through covetousness shall they with feigned words make merchandise of you: whose judgment now of a long time lingereth not, and their damnation slumbereth not." The modernist covets the salary paid by Bible-believing Christians, hence he pretends to be a Christian when he is not, pretends to be a gospel minister when he is a minister of Satan. Modernists "make merchandise" of simple, Bible-believing Christians. They deceive the people to hold their jobs and to have the money and honor that belong to honest Christian leaders. These wolves want the support of sheep, so they put on sheep's clothing. These false prophets want the money for their schools, the money for their denominational headquarters, which Bible-believing Christians give to Jesus Christ. So, like the hypocrites that they are, for covetousness' sake they make merchandise of Christians!

How can anyone respect the modernist preacher who takes vows that he does not intend to keep, who professes a Christianity in which he does not believe?

A weak Christian may be pitied, may be lovingly for-given. The ignorant Christian should have the forbear-ance and help of Christians. A lost sinner who admits he is a lost sinner may be lovingly warned and perhaps won by those who love the Lord Jesus. But the modern-ist, who is not a Christian in the historical sense, but claims to be; who does not believe the Bible but pretends to preach it; who is an infidel, an unbeliever, but hides it in order to have the honor and support of Christians, can have only the scorn reserved for hypocrites!

Modernists Dishonest in Not Seeking the Truth About Christ and the Bible

When a man deceives the people and stays in the church when he is an infidel, then such a man's motives are not to be trusted.

And you may be sure that even the way a man became a modernist, an infidel, was not an honest way. Modern-ists are not honest doubters.

I do not mean that the modernist is not a doubter; I mean that he did not come to his doubts by honest means. Modernists are doubters, but not honest doubters. Re-member that Jesus said, "O fools, and *slow of heart* to believe all that the prophets have spoken." Modernists do not believe the Bible because their hearts are wrong. They did not find the truth because they did not honestly, with an open heart, seek the truth.

There is a clear doctrine that runs throughout the Bible, teaching that one who honestly seeks God can find Him, one who wants to know the truth can find it. In Jeremiah 29: 13 we are told, "And ye shall seek me, and find me, when ye shall search for me with all your heart." Notice that a certain heart attitude is necessary to find God. The heart cannot certainly know the truth in spiritual things when the heart is rebellious against God.

In John 7: 17 Jesus said, "If any man willeth to do his will, he shall know of the teaching, whether it is of God, or whether I speak from myself" (R.V.). Any man who is willing to do the will of God when it is revealed can find out whether Christ is the Son of God, whether the Bible is the infallible revelation of God, or not. The same truth is taught in James 4: 8, "Draw nigh to God, and he will draw nigh to you."

I have taken God up on these promises and I found that the Bible is true. Modernists have not honestly, with an open heart, sought to know whether the Bible is true.

People Believe in Evolution Instead of the Bible, Not Because of Scientific Proof, But by Choice

High school teachers and others with a little learning may say that "Evolution is a proved fact of science." Of course, real men of science make no such claim. Let me assure you, as a man of good university training, a former college teacher, an editor and author, that all scientists know that evolution is not a proved fact. No honest and responsible scientist in the whole world will say that the teaching of evolution is more than a theory, an hypothesis, a guess. There is no proof to evolution.

Not one case in all the world is known of the origin of a single clearly separate species by evolution.

Not one example has ever been found in which an animal or plant was clearly evolved from one species to another species. There is not one single proof that man, in inherent physical and mental equipment, has changed from prehistoric times until now.

On the contrary, there is all about us the evidence of design in nature that points back to a personal Creator. The God who gave man lungs made air for him to breathe. The God who made man's eyes made light so he could see. The God who made man's ears made the physical laws of sound. In every human body are a thousand evidences of creation by a God who was infinitely wise and infinitely good. All the real evidence is on the side of creation by a supernatural God instead of evolution by inherent forces.

Why, then, do people believe in evolution? Of course the mass of people who believe it do so because they are taught to believe it and they want to believe it because it is the accepted thing. But why do scientists, educators, believe in evolution? The answer still is that they want to believe it.

Dr. Bateman, in a presidential address at a meeting of the Association for the Advancement of Science at Toronto some years ago, reviewed the unpleasant (to him) fact that evolution was far from proved and that many ideas scientists had taken for granted in connection with the evolutionary hypothesis were now proved untenable. But he still said that evolution must be true because the only alternative to evolution was direct creation of God, which he certainly would not accept. In other words, Dr. Bateman believed in evolution, contrary to the evidence, because he did not want to believe in direct creation!

Men who doubt the Bible have gone to every possible trouble and expense to try to prove evolution. Hundreds of generations of white mice and guinea pigs have been used in trying to bring about some clearly defined departure from the original species, but without success. Cattle have been bred to buffaloes, and it was once announced that Colonel Goodnight of Texas had developed a new strain, "cattaloes." But the so-called new species simply bred back to buffalo and cattle. Scientists have tried to find mules that would reproduce. An effort was even made to mix Africans with chimpanzees. Life cells have been treated with X-rays and radium and electric shock. Still no new species have appeared.

Scientists have combed the world for a skeleton or a living creature that could be called the missing link between man and apes. Scientists have used a small piece of jawbone and a bit of a skull with a leg bone, probably not even of the same individual, and have, with much plaster, unveiled a skeleton to satisfy their needs. A faked picture was widely published of a native Filipino said to have been born with a long tail; but it was proved a fake.

The fact still remains that the link is still missing. An infinite gulf remains between mankind and the most complex and advanced beasts in the world.

A missing link? All the links are missing! There is no link between inanimate matter and living matter, organic and inorganic. We have no link between plants

and animals. We have no link between conscious life
and unconscious. We have no link between man and
beast. In fact, we have no link between any two well-
defined species in the world.

You see, men do not accept evolution because the facts
force them to accept it. They accept it because they want
to, in spite of the facts.

Evolutionists string a million guesses together and
come out with only a theory, but they believe it in spite
of the evidence.

Darwin said that man was descended from the apes.
Now it is proved that that could not possibly be so, and
no scientist today believes in "Darwinian evolution." The
difference in blood cells, chromosomes, etc., makes it certain man did not descend from any creature living today,
and scientists so admit it, but they still believe in
evolution!

Darwin said that evolution was affected by so-called
"natural selection"; now no reputable scientist will risk
his reputation on that silly theory. They do not believe
now, as Darwin did, that giraffes grew long necks in a
period of drought, reaching high to eat leaves off the
trees! They do not believe now, as Darwin taught, that
the hair largely disappeared from men's bodies because
the females would not marry the hairy men and so they
had no children and a hairless race developed!

The teaching of evolution was originally based on
the idea that acquired characteristics were transmitted to
offspring. Now we know this is not true. Sheep, descended from a thousand generations of sheep with their
tails cut off, still grow long tails and likewise have them

cut off. Jewish boy babies, despite thirty-five centuries of circumcision, are born unchanged.

But do all these discoveries discourage the evolutionists? No, because they want to believe in evolution and they do not want to believe the Bible.

Once modernists said that Moses could not have written the Pentateuch because men could not read and write in Moses' day. Now no educated man who knows of the Tel el Amarna tablets and other modern discoveries can doubt that men of Moses' day wrote. On a thousand fronts modernists have been driven back as clay tablets and stone inscriptions and the uncovered ruins of ancient cities proved the modernists wrong. There was a nation of Hittites, though the modernists long said there were none. Cyrenius was governor of Syria briefly, as Luke 2:2 declares—as historians now know, but once denied. Not one archaeological discovery, not one ancient manuscript, not one scientific development has disproved a single statement of the Word of God. Yet modernists go blithely and determinedly on their way opposing it.

Why do modernists still not believe the Bible? Because they do not want to believe it! If the Bible were true, then men ought to follow it. If the Ten Commandments be God's laws, then murder, adultery, lying and covetousness will be punished and sinful men will be held accountable for their sins. If there be a Hell for God-rejecting sinners, then these men who hate Christ are in danger of eternal damnation, and they do not like such a doctrine. If Christ be the virgin-born Son of God, then they ought to love Him and trust Him and serve and obey Him. Don't you see how modernists who

want to live for today instead of eternity, who want to
have their own way instead of God's way, who want to
be popular with men instead of righteous before God,
hate the Bible?

The Blindness, the Unbelief of Modernists, Is Caused by a Wicked Heart Attitude Against God

The Bible, wonderful Book of God, reveals the heart
of wicked men.   In II Peter 3: 5 God tells us that modernists are willingly ignorant of the true creation of the
heavens and earth.   Read the whole passage carefully:

*"Knowing this first, that there shall come in the last
days scoffers, walking after their own lusts, And saying,
Where is the promise of his coming? for since the fathers
fell asleep, all things continue as they were from the
beginning of the creation. For this they willingly are
ignorant of, that by the word of God the heavens were
of old, and the earth standing out of the water and in
the water: Whereby the world that then was, being overflowed with water, perished"* (II Pet. 3: 3-6).

Are there men who do not believe "that by the word of
God the heavens were of old, and the earth standing out
of the water and in the water"?   Are there men who do
not believe the Bible account of the flood, that "the world
that then was, being overflowed with water, perished"?
Then these men, false prophets to "come in the last days,"
are really "scoffers, walking after their own lusts." They
believe their false doctrines because they want to believe
them.   "They willingly are ignorant," says the Scripture, of the true creation of the heaven and earth by the
Word of God.   "They willingly are ignorant" of the

flood which overflowed the world in the days of Noah.

Those who do not believe in true creation are ignorant, and choose to remain ignorant. When they scoff at the Bible they simply walk after their own lusts, their own heart's desires.

I suggest that you read the above Scripture again carefully and see how aptly it describes these modernist fools, these hypocrites who do not want to believe the Bible. They desire to please men and not God. They desire a religion that does not require repentance, does not call for a new birth, does not threaten punishment for sin. There is a fundamental hypocrisy, a sinfulness of motive back of all unbelief in the Bible and Christ.

Modernists are doubters, but not honest doubters.

It has become true of all modernists as Romans 1:21, 22 says:

"Because that, when they knew God, they glorified him not as God, neither were thankful; but became vain in their imaginations, and their foolish heart was darkened. Professing themselves to be wise, they became fools."

In Romans 1:24 we are told about certain sinful men, "Wherefore God also gave them up to uncleanness . . ." and in verse 26, "For this cause God gave them up unto vile affections." In verse 28 we are told, "And even as they did not like to retain God in their knowledge, God gave them over to a reprobate mind."

The blindness, the folly of modernists, is the result of their wicked hearts. Unbelief is not a product of the mind, but of the heart. Unbelief does not come from intelligent investigation; it comes from sin in the heart.

They are "slow of heart" to believe, even as Jesus said in Luke 24: 25.

Every modernist may insist that he is perfectly honest in his stand. He may have a conviction, but it is not a conviction based on honest investigation. He may doubt the Bible, but it is not the honest doubt of one who could not find evidence. Modernists turn from the Bible, not because they find the Bible unbelievable, but because they do not want to believe it. Modernists turn from Christ, not because He is not willing to prove Himself all He claims to be, but because they simply do not want Him as God's perfect Saviour. I do not even say that modernists do not want to know the truth. Some of them do want to know the truth, but not at the cost of displeasing men and repenting of their sins and surrendering their lives. The fault is a heart fault. Modernists are wrong in the head because they were first wrong in their wills, their hearts.

So when you meet a modernist, remember Jesus said he is a wolf in sheep's clothing; that he comes in privily, bringing damnable heresies, denying the Lord that bought him, and that he brings feigned words because of his covetousness, hoping to make merchandise of Bible-believing Christians, as we are told in II Peter 2: 1-3. He is "willingly ignorant" of the truth, as II Peter 3: 3-6 says. The modernist is a hypocrite.

VI. The Modernist Is Under an Awful Curse From God and From Christ

In Galatians 1: 8, 9, Paul said by divine inspiration:

"But though we, or an angel from heaven, preach any other gospel unto you than that which we have preached unto you, let him be accursed.   As we said before, so say I now again, If any man preach any other gospel unto you than that ye have received, let him be accursed."

To Teach Any Gospel Except Salvation Through Christ's Death Puts One Under God's Curse

You can see that the Scripture above refers to modernists who do not preach the gospel of salvation by personal faith in Christ and His atoning death, but teach salvation by human merit or worth or works.   Paul tells us in I Corinthians 15: 1, 3, 4 what his gospel was:

"Moreover, brethren, I declare unto you the gospel which I preached unto you . . . how that Christ died for our sins according to the scriptures: And that he was buried, and that he rose again the third day according to the scriptures."

Those who do not believe in the atoning death of Christ, in His bodily resurrection and in salvation through His blood, preach another gospel.   And by God's inspiration, Paul says that such a one is accursed, under damnation.

The awful curse of God is on all modernists.

As we have shown you before, the modernist is an infidel, not a Christian, not a believer.

The modernist is an insincere hypocrite who, because of his sinful heart, would not seek the truth honestly nor submit to the Word of God nor follow the light he had. For this reason God has turned him over to a darkened heart and a reprobate mind.   Light rejected means light

withdrawn.   So the modernist is under a curse as a
lost sinner, as an infidel, and as a willful hypocrite, deceiving the people for covetousness' sake.   How terrible
is God's curse upon him!

Christians have a solemn duty in this connection. Second John 7-11 says:

*"For many deceivers are entered into the world, who
confess not that Jesus Christ is come in the flesh. This
is a deceiver and an antichrist. Look to yourselves, that
we lose not those things which we have wrought, but
that we receive a full reward. Whosoever transgresseth,
and abideth not in the doctrine of Christ, hath not God.
He that abideth in the doctrine of Christ, he hath both
the Father and the Son. If there come any unto you,
and bring not this doctrine, receive him not into your
house, neither bid him God speed: For he that biddeth
him God speed is partaker of his evil deeds."*

Modernists do not agree that Jesus is the pre-existent
Christ of the Old Testament, the one foretold by the
prophets, the Christ of God. Everyone who does not accept Christ as God come in the flesh according to prophecy, is a deceiver and an antichrist, says the Scripture.
And Christians are to look to themselves carefully lest
they lose their reward for their works and suffer because
of compromising with these unbelievers and modernists.
One who does not abide in the doctrine of Christ, the
Christ of the Bible, does not have God, is not a Christian,
is not to be received as a Christian.

It is a sin for a Christian not to have fellowship with
other born-again Christians. But it is equally a sin for
Christians to fellowship with infidels as Christians.

Christians Must Not Fellowship With Nor Support Modernists

Then we have the clear command of II John, verses 10 and 11: "If there come any unto you, and bring not this doctrine, receive him not into your house, neither bid him God speed: For he that biddeth him God speed is partaker of his evil deeds." Christians are not to receive a modernist into their homes. It is a sin for a Christian to receive a modernist as a Christian. It is a sin for a Christian to support the modernist with his money. It is a sin for a Christian even to bid the modernist God speed in his preaching and teaching. Everyone who gives a dime to support a modernist, or allows his influence to be used in approval of a modernist who denies part of the Bible, is a partaker of the infidel's evil deeds. If the reader is a Christian who compromises with modernists and supports them, this Scripture warns you that you will lose part of your reward in Heaven. In Christ's dear name, do not receive a modernist as a Christian, do not go to hear a modernist preach, do not send your child to schools where people teach who claim to be Christians but deny part of the Bible.

Modernists are under the curse of God! Christians should fear them, avoid them, withdraw support from them and pray for them!

VII. The Remedy for Modernism; How to Become Convinced Concerning the Bible and Christ and Salvation

Every honest unbeliever who wants to know the truth

can find it. I remind you again that Jesus said, "If any man willeth to do his will, he shall know of the teaching, whether it is of God, or whether I speak from myself" (John 7: 17 R.V.). James 4: 8 says, "Draw nigh to God, and he will draw nigh to you." Another Scripture says, "Then shall we know, if we follow on to know the Lord" (Hos. 6: 3). One who honestly sets out to find the truth about the Bible and Christ and salvation can find it. But one must seek honestly with a whole heart. Jeremiah 29: 13 says, "And ye shall seek me, and find me, when ye shall search for me with all your heart."

Honest, Penitent Hearts Can Find the Truth

Dr. R. A. Torrey was wonderfully used of God in winning atheists to Christ. Again and again he challenged men if they were honest to set out honestly to find God by humble prayer, reading of the Scripture, by honest surrender and decision to follow what light God would give them. Some men would not search the Scripture, would not pray to God for light, would not agree to follow the Bible if they found it true and to receive Christ as Saviour if they found Him the Son of God. Such men, of course, had no help from God. But honest, surrendered, penitent hearts can always find the light and the truth and salvation.

John 20: 31 tells us that the Bible, and particularly the Gospel of John, was written "that ye might believe that Jesus is the Christ, the Son of God: and that believing ye might have life through his name." It is clear, then, that any honest heart who wants to know the truth about Christ as the Son of God and about the Bible as the Word of God, should set out to read prayerfully through the Gospel of John and other Scripture, seeking for light.

It is equally certain that anyone honestly seeking God ought penitently to confess and forsake his sins. Remember, unbeliever, that your trouble is with your heart, not with your head. Until your heart turns honestly in simple repentance from your sins, God has no promise that He will meet you or reveal Himself to you. You are to seek God 'with your whole heart.'

A Christian lawyer talked to an infidel lawyer who said he could not believe that the Bible was truly the Word of God, could not believe that Christ was veritably the virgin-born Son of God. Said the Christian lawyer:

"Let me prepare a brief of the evidence, proving that the Bible is the Word of God and that Christ is God's own Son. I have evidence that would be acceptable in any court of law. Will you read such a brief of the evidence carefully, if I prepare it?"

The unsaved infidel lawyer agreed, and in due time the arguments were briefly written out and submitted.

Later the infidel lawyer saw his Christian friend and said, "You are right! Your arguments have proved to me beyond a doubt that the Bible is God's Word and that Christ is God's Son. So I am convinced that it is all so."

"Praise the Lord!" said the Christian lawyer. "I am so happy to see you turn to God."

"Wait a minute!" said the unsaved lawyer. "I said that I am convinced that the Bible is the Word of God and that Christ is God's Son. I am sure you are right about that. But though I find the Bible is the Word of God, I still do not want to follow it. Though I believe that Christ is the Son of God, I still am not ready to take Him as my Saviour."

You see, what is wrong with an infidel is not his head but his heart. In that case the unbeliever was able to see the truth of the Bible, even while his heart was impenitent. But God makes no promise to give light and understanding to impenitent sinners. Unless you are willing to confess your pride and willfulness, willing to turn from your sin and look to Christ for forgiveness and salvation, willing to set out to live for Christ, there is no promise that you will find the truth. If you are determined to go to Hell anyhow, I think God would just as soon you should go to Hell as an infidel as to have you go as a Bible believer but still a lost sinner. Why should God fix your poor, deluded head when your wicked heart does not surrender to Him? Remember that it is always sin that makes infidels and modernists, and humble repentance is always the cure for what is wrong with a sinner.

How I Know the Bible Is True

Let me give a word of personal testimony here. In 1921 I went to the University of Chicago to do graduate work. I had taught the preceding season at Wayland College, Plainview, Texas, and had a contract to teach the next year in another college. I had been converted in childhood and had lived as a Christian. I believed the Bible, but strangely enough had also accepted the theory of evolution. I came to see that the teaching of the Bible and the teaching that this universe, plants, animals and mankind and even Christianity, were simply the products of evolution, are simply irreconcilable. If man came by natural evolution, he did not come by direct creation. If Christianity came by true revelation of God in the Bible, then it did not grow from human superstition. So, with some fear and trembling, but with an honest heart, I vowed that I would know the truth.

William Jennings Bryan came to the University of Chicago and spoke on "The Bible and Its Enemies." If Bryan and other Bible believers, including my own godly father and mother, were right, then the evolutionists, the modernists, the unbelievers, were wrong. But if the evolutionists and modernists were right, if the Bible were full of mistakes, if Christ were only a good man, then I determined I would know it. I would not be a hypocrite. I would not pretend to believe what I did not believe. I would not claim to be a Christian in faith if I could not honestly be one.

I thank God that the search that followed proved to me beyond any possible doubt that the Bible is the Word of God, infallibly accurate, as given in the original manuscripts (and the present translations are almost perfect reproductions of those manuscripts). I found that the Bible is authenticated by hundreds of prophecies fulfilled to the letter. I found that it is absolutely reliable in science and history. I found that the only people who do not believe the Bible are those who never set out with an honest, seeking heart to know the whole truth and to trust and follow the Christ of the Bible and please and serve the God who has revealed Himself there. On this matter I am not guessing, nor hoping. I *know* by my own researches, by facts I have at hand that would convince any honest investigator, that the Bible is all it claims to be, the very Word of God, and that Christ is all He claims to be, God incarnate, the virgin-born, bodily-resurrected Son of God, the Saviour of all who trust in Him.   Now for long years I have acted on the assumption that the Bible is true, and the Word of God has proved itself.   I have risked the support of my family, my reputation, my happiness, even my life—yea, my soul itself—on the literal promises found in the Word of God.   Thousands of times I have found that God does exactly what He promises to do in the Bible.   What God says will happen does happen when one meets His requirements.

I have proved the Bible is true by preaching it to sinners and I have seen the gospel of the Bible transform the lives of multiplied thousands.   Hundreds of drunkards have been made sober, harlots have been made pure and virtuous, convicts have been made into respectable and trustworthy citizens.   The timid have been made bold, the sad have been made happy.   Better than I have proved any friend on earth I have proved the Bible.   I have better proof that the Bible is the perfect Word of God than I have of the honor of any man, the virtue of any woman.

Acting on clear promises in the Bible, I gave up position, salary, ten thousand dollars of life insurance, when intelligent, sensible people said I would come to want and my family would go hungry.   Thank God, with no set salary, putting no price on my service, giving away thousands of dollars, I have been wonderfully cared for, with my large family, for twenty-one years!   Once after prayer I adopted a course, true to the Word of God, which good men told me could drive me from the ministry and bring me to shame and my family to want. But God did just what He said He would do in the Bible and came to my rescue. I have *proved* the Bible. It works! I know that the Bible is true, as I know the multiplication table is true. And as literally multiplied thousands of other Christians have, I have by honest testing gone from doubting to knowing and from fear to certainty, from unbelief to faith.

Unbeliever, Will You Seek God Today?

A last word and I am done. In a Texas town where I was preaching in a revival campaign a newspaper reporter declared that he had too much education, that he was too modern and rational and had too much information, to believe the Bible.

"How can I help it," he asked, "if I cannot believe?"

But I found that he had not as much education as I had. He had been reading from Haldeman-Julian trash and thought he had found an alibi for his sins!

So I said to the young infidel something like this:

"You do not know whether the Bible is true or not, but I do know. Your father, your mother, and millions of other Christians have tried it and found that Christ does save, that the Bible is true, that it works in daily life. Now I challenge you. I know you can find out whether Christianity is true. I know *how* you can find out. I am going to tell you how, and then if you do not seek to know the truth I will know that you are a hypocrite, your brother here will know that you are insincere, that you do not know the truth and you do not want to know it. Are you willing to seek the truth honestly and follow it if you find it?"

He replied that of course he would like to know the truth, but believed it was impossible to know about such a matter.

I said, "Are you willing to kneel, then, here with me and ask God, if there be a God, to clear up your mind on this matter and make you able to see and acknowledge the truth? If God shows you that the Bible is true, will you set out to live by it at any cost? If it becomes clear to you that Christ is the Son of God, that He died on the cross to save you from sin, it is obvious that you ought to love Him and trust Him and give Him your heart, now and forever. Are you willing to do it?"

He argued. How could he pray to God when he didn't even know if there were a God? But I insisted that an honest God would keep His promises if any honest heart sought to know the truth and follow it.

At last he turned to his brother and said, "Bud, we will have to do it! We cannot claim to be honest if we do not give God a chance to prove Himself to us."

So we three knelt together. I prayed first, telling God how this young man had gone in his proud way, living in sin, reading infidel literature and saying that the Bible was not true. I asked my heavenly Father to open this lost sinner's heart and give him a conviction of the truth. Then I asked the young newspaper reporter to pray. I asked him to admit that he was a sinner who needed forgiveness and light.

Stumblingly he began to pray. Words came slowly.

He asked God, if there were a God, to reveal Himself. He asked that if there were such a God He would forgive this sinner. He promised if light came that he would follow it. Suddenly he broke into sobbing! He turned to me and admitted that it was all settled. His doubts were all gone. As soon as he penitently surrendered to and trusted in Jesus Christ, his infidelity was gone. His trouble was his sin, not his intelligence.

A good many professed infidels have been saved in my services. I know that every man and woman in the world who wants to know the truth can know it, provided he will first turn from his own sins with confession and repentance and then set out to follow the light when God gives it, whether through His Word or through the Holy Spirit.

To remain a modernist, to deny Christ's deity and His atoning death and to reject the gospel of salvation as given in the Bible, means that you must go to Hell. Oh, do not remain in that sin of unbelief! Turn your face toward the light today. Follow on to know the light and God will give it! Every doubter in the world who is willing to seek God with all his heart will have his head trouble cured when his heart is changed.

Let every reader try to see that this message is read by some one who claims not to believe the Bible.

TWELVE TREMENDOUS THEMES

BY DR. JOHN R. RICE

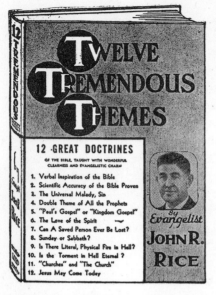

12 GREAT DOCTRINES
OF THE BIBLE, TAUGHT WITH WONDERFUL
CLEARNESS AND EVANGELISTIC CHARM

1. Verbal Inspiration of the Bible
2. Scientific Accuracy of the Bible Proven
3. The Universal Malady, Sin
4. Double Theme of All the Prophets
5. "Paul's Gospel" or "Kingdom Gospel"
6. The Love of the Spirit
7. Can A Saved Person Ever Be Lost?
8. Sunday or Sabbath?
9. Is There Literal, Physical Fire in Hell?
10. Is the Torment in Hell Eternal ?
11. "Churches" and "The Church"
12. Jesus May Come Today

By Evangelist **JOHN R. RICE**

Fifteen years ago Dr. Rice began systematic Bible study and began his written ministry. In this book he has selected the twelve most important themes of rich, doctrinal Bible teaching written in fifteen years. These 'TWELVE TREMENDOUS THEMES' cover the inspiration of the Bible, sin, salvation, the work of the Holy Spirit, security, law vs. grace, the Bible teaching about the bride and body of Christ, and also about local congregations, and about the second coming of Christ. Here is a whole Bible course in itself, a tremendous book which we believe will be one of the most popular Dr. Rice ever wrote. Note the chapter titles in picture.

Introduction by Robert G. Lee, D.D., L.L.D., Litt.D., Pastor Bellevue Baptist Church, Memphis, Tennessee. Dr. Lee says:

"I have read the manuscript with delight and with profit and with prayer that it will have a wide circulation. Such a book is needed and will, when read and preached, do unmeasurable good in this day of invertebrate theology, jelly-fish morality, India - rubber convictions, see - saw philosophy, scientific conceit—when some speak with breath strong with conjectural onions and foul with the garlic of critical contempt for Scriptural certainties.

"This book is truth simply and pungently phrased. It sets forth conclusions clearly and concisely expressed. It is declaration saturated and foundationed with the Scriptures. It makes appeal wooingly and earnestly uttered. This book is real bread and meat for the strengthening of Christians, real milk for nourishing the Christian, honey for sweetening the Christian, fire for warming the Christian. Those who read it and lay hold of its truths will know that it is stimulation for the sluggard, stirring for the complacent, anchorage for the unstable, courage for the timid, insistence for the undecided.

"This book honors God, honors the Christ who is God, honors the Holy Spirit, honors the church, honors the Gospel, warns the wicked, invites the sinner to accept Christ—and comforts all who believe the Bible to be the inspired, infallible, inerrant Word of God."

These 'TWELVE TREMENDOUS THEMES' arm the young Christian against Modernism, against the doctrine of salvation by good works, against ultra-dispensationalism, against modern cults who would break down belief in an eternal Hell taught by the Bible. It gives the most important teaching about the work of the Holy Spirit and about the second coming of Christ.

177 extra large pages. A tremendous book of nearly 100,000 words, beautifully clothbound, attractive jacket. Price only **$1.50**